WHEN IT COMES
TO FORGIVING
YOU...

By
Natalie Rose Kohuth

To Debbie,
Peace of heart is
a grace of God. May
all you do be guided
by God's grace, love,
and mercy!
Natalie Rose
Watson

Copyright © 2013, Natalie Rose Kohuth

ISBN 978-1483930909

When It Comes to Forgiving You
By: Natalie Kohuth

"When it comes to forgiving you,
I fall a little short,
my attempts are a little flat.
Cause I'm waiting around for a knife in the
back.

And you know it's not okay,
you can't find the right words to say,
can't change it now.
I gave you a chance to take things back.

So now I'm taking my turn,
I took a walk around,
you'll never guess what I learned.
Picked myself up and I'm not looking back.

I'm staring in the mirror,
smiling, no more tears,
took the time and calmed the fears.
Carrying on and I haven't looked back."

Acknowledgements

The biggest Thank You to Tom Bird for making all of this a reality. Without you, I would have never gotten this far, let alone had the opportunity in the first place.

Thank you to Mrs. Mokay for helping me through the hard times, and being part of the process.

Thank you to my mother, Grama and Pap, Alex, and the rest of my true family and friends for helping me be the person I am.

In Loving Memory of Mack, the greatest German Shepherd in Heaven.

Chapter 1

Why can't I sleep? I'm tired. It's late. I should be able to, but no. I haven't been able to sleep well for days on end. I look across the room to the other bed. My younger sister Anna is sleeping soundly. She'll continue to sleep like this for hours. I'll be lucky if I get to sleep at all.

Then I start to listen. Down the hall I can hear the sound of Gabriel's music playing. Aside from that, his loud snoring drowns out almost everything else. If I listen hard, I can hear the soft sound of the television in my mother's room. She keeps it turned down so it wouldn't disturb us with the noise. I focus on my favorite sound. Our dog Shadow is in the kitchen downstairs. I imagine the sound of his toenails against the ceramic tile floor. It is too soft to hear from my room.

"Good dog," I think towards the animal. Shadow starts up the stairs to make his nightly rounds. He goes from room, to room checking on his sleeping family. To me, it seems his life is consumed with my family, and mostly with our health and safety. Finally the big German Shepherd pushes into Anna and my room. Shadow finds that I'm awake and takes that opportunity to climb in bed with me. He curls beside me and within minutes; I am able to fall asleep.

Sleep is so peaceful. It's almost like you're able to escape the world all together. It's like a mini vacation every night. All too soon it ends, unfortunately. When I open my eyes, I am blinded by the bright sunlight coming through the window.

I look across the room and find Anna has already gone downstairs for the day. Of course, the youngest gets up early on the weekends. In my opinion, the weekends were created for sleep. My nose wrinkles as I take in the amount of perfume she has used this morning.

When Anna turned ten, she became obsessed with acting older. She feels she should drown her body with heavy scents. At least my make-up bag looks intact today.

One time she had used it without my help or permission. I was yelled at for the outcome. It looked as if a clown had gotten excited and thrown up on her face. That's what I get for leaving my things in easy reach.

I crawl out of bed and change clothes before heading downstairs for breakfast. Noise greets me as I enter the kitchen. I missed most of the excitement.

"Mom, I need more eggs," Anna insists. This makes me smile, I swear that girl would eat herself sick if she was allowed. I find Gabriel in the corner nibbling on a piece of bacon. He is always so quiet in the mornings. Gabriel is the oldest of the three of us. His 16th birthday had just passed last week.

It always amazed me, Gabriel's personality that is. He is either calm and laid back, or aggressive and quick to act. It's like two different people are fighting to control him constantly. He hides it well though. He learned young. Always benefits and draw backs to being older. Right now, I wanted to prove I could be as quiet and calm as he usually was.

Don't get me wrong, I'm not a trouble maker. Gabriel is by no one's standards the angel he's named after. He is just good at keeping calm so there's less stress in the house. I respect him for it. I know I could never just sit there and...

"Hope, aren't you gonna eat?" Anna asked around a mouth full of eggs.

"Sure," I say, even though I'm not that hungry. No use in skipping the most important meal of the day. I'd only be reminded about it for the rest of the day anyway.

Luckily, our mom recently got over her experimental kitchen phase. She would add and mix random combinations of foods together that would've been better separate. Recently, she started cooking normally again and we were all happy. Even my mom's boyfriend had complained that the food was a bit extreme. He never complains; which is probably the main reason for the shift to normal recipes. Whatever the reason, I'm thankful.

At one point in time, we had actually gone down the road to our grandparents house and knocked on the door. When they answered, we faked tears and choked out sobs and begged for food. We stayed for dinner and got a roast with green beans from the garden.

Gabriel's phone goes off, he looks at the name of the caller and groans. I know that face well, too well. Only one thing causes him to react this way. Mom recognizes it as well. This is one of the things that is able to set Gabriel off. His gray eyes darken and his muscles tense. I hear his voice and am surprised it is not the razor-sharp tone I expect, instead it is forced politeness. You can barely detect the hatred behind his facade.

The call is quick. At points it seems he had to make a mental note not to snarl into the phone. The call ends and Gabriel snaps his phone shut. He takes a deep breath and lays it on the table. He lets out a loud exhale before speaking.

'Dad called," now his words were daggers. "He'll be here at noon to take us out for our time together this weekend."

It was strange, usually we had to call our dad several times before, he answered us. We tried to make arrangements before and it usually failed. Many times he ditched us all together, no call to say that he wouldn't be seeing us. No regrets, no excuse. Like he had something so much better to do in his life. Because in his eyes, blowing off your children wouldn't cause the problems that it did.

"How long is he taking us?" I asked. I didn't want to be there longer than needed. I didn't want to plaster a happy-go-lucky smile to my face and pretend that my skin didn't crawl when I sat within ten feet of him.

"No clue, probably the same as usual, an hour or two before we bore him." Gabriel said, "That or he feels his paternal duties have been satisfied."

I felt bad now. I saw how much Gabriel hated to go with our dad. He hated making it seem as if everything was alright when it clearly wasn't. Most of the time we were there, we acted as if nothing was wrong. To our dad, it was like an hour or two of time spent together every once in a while made him a better person. As if anything possibly could.

Anna cleared the table, intent on being a huge help. She wanted to know where Dad was taking us and questioned her brother about it. Gabriel left the room without answering. Leave it to the little one to make him storm off. The anger wasn't directed at Anna, but she still hung her head upset. At least, he left before he said something that he would regret later.

Mom was stressed now. Sometimes she got that way easily. At times she would yell at Gabriel, as if he were the cause to how things were. Gabriel couldn't stand it but didn't fight back. When he wasn't around, the burden fell on my shoulders. But what use would it be to fight back? Why cause more tension? Sit there and take it, that's what I learned after listening to Gabriel take harsh words fueled by anger that had nothing to do with him.

I didn't mind as much as Gabriel did because I understood better. Her anger wasn't because of us. We didn't cause it. It was the only way our mom vented though. I took it because I would rather a few stray comments not affect me than let it build up. I stood my ground and took what I already knew was coming.

"Why does he have to be that way?" she had tears streaming from her eyes. "I know he doesn't enjoy spending quality time with your dad. I understand that. God knows I understand that. Why does he have to take it out on this family though?"

I wanted to defend my brother. I debated on what to say.

My mother continued, "he's all calm, then something happens dealing with your father and he goes off like that. Doesn't he see that I can't control it? I can't make your father a better person, I tried for years and nothing helped him."

This was not Gabriel going off. This was him preventing himself from going off on the people he cared about. Mom didn't see this. She saw it as him being rude to her and not caring about what he did or said.

I walked over to my mom. Somehow I wanted to comfort her. I hated seeing her so upset. I put my hand on her shoulder and she pushed away, leaving the room.

Anna looked even more upset now. Tears overflowed and fell from her eyes. She came over to me and hugged me. My poor little sister cried softly in my arms. I didn't want her to think the one sided argument had been her fault, but I couldn't think of anything to make the situation any better in her eyes.

"Why do Gabriel and mommy have to fight?" she whimpered. Anna may be ten, but when she is sad or upset she is a little girl all over again. All I saw was a very strong young girl. A little girl who I would've traded anything for her never having to deal with the things my brother and I dealt with. There was nothing either of us could do though.

"They were just upset," how do I explain?

"At each other?" She looked puzzled.

"No, not at all, daddy stresses Gabe and he gets mad, that's all sweety. Mom just wants him to be happy. Sometimes she gets stressed when things don't happen that way." Anna seemed content with the knowledge that she wasn't the heart of the conflict and left to get ready for our dad.

I looked at the clock to check the time. There was forty-five minutes before we had to leave. I was already dressed and ready, so I went to find Gabriel. On the way to his room, I passed my mom doing a load of laundry. Her eyes were still red, but she seemed better. The small incident all but forgotten.

I knock softly at Gabriel's door. The music flicked off and the door opened shortly after.

"What do you want?" he asked coldly. He didn't usually snap. Usually he tried to be extra nice to Anna and me. He realized he'd been out of place. "Sorry. You know I just can't take him sometimes. I hate the nice act. It drives me crazy."

"I know, the only one who can stand him is Anna, but that doesn't really say much. She's too young to remember anything. There's no way she'd remember how he was. Everything to her is rough at best."

Gabriel scoffed. He knew Anna didn't understand how bad our dad was. I was only two years younger than Gabriel and he knew that his feelings would not be a hassle for me. That was why we got along so well, we talked to each other whenever something like this came up.

He opened his door wide enough to let me in. His form of an invitation. I enter and almost tripped over the mess in his room. There wasn't any clutter in the middle of the room, but along the walls, boxes and other objects were stacked high. I also noticed there was an increase in the number of posters that he hung on the wall. The window was open, cleaning the air in the room.

Plopping down on the computer chair I looked up at him. I know most siblings find it natural to fight, but we've been through too much together to allow the stupid things to get to us. The rare times a fight does occur, it isn't over who ate the last cookie, or who was allowed to pick what to watch on T.V.

I don't like to admit it, but I am proud of Gabriel. He tries to protect us. He wants to make sure Anna doesn't have to go through everything we went through. He never wants Anna or me to deal with what Mom had to go through with a man. He sits there waiting for me to talk.

At times I felt sorry for Gabe. I knew he felt betrayed by our dad. They had been close, or at least Gabriel had assumed they were. He was the only son, so often they would spend evenings playing together. Father and son time was a must for the pair. They'd play ball or go fishing in the lake that was accessible through the woods next to the house. On special occasions they would drive out to a golf range and spend hours there messing around and practicing.

I watched him a moment longer before talking, "What set you off?" I asked.

He clenched his fists but relaxed quickly. This was accompanied by another loud exhale.

"I don't even know anymore. Every time I'm around him, or talk to him, he acts likes he's so pleased. Like he feels like he's a good dad. As if he made a good difference in our lives. I don't like the tone he uses with me. Like we're friends."

I frowned, "we already know he's not here for us."

Gabriel is fast to come back, "We already know, we already know, I know! So why can't I get over the fact that he's not here?"

I waited til he wasn't so red.

"We have to…" I started but decided against it. Truth was, we did have to go see our dad. That didn't mean he felt he had the time to see us. That didn't mean he cared about us enough to come and see us, or even call for that matter. He's gone months, literally without even so much as a phone call.

"We set ourselves up for it." I said.

"I just want you and Anna to have a chance at a dad," he whispered. He put his head down in his hands. Gabriel was more of a dad to us than our real one. "I'm past that chance. I gave it up years ago. I just don't want either of you to feel like this. To feel like your missing something. We all lost something when there was nothing there to lose in the first place."

Years ago we had decided that we no longer wanted to even see our dad. After waiting so long we just gave up on the dream that he'd become a better person and a good parent. Anna still wanted the chance to see him. She still wanted the chance to have a father. All because she didn't see what we were able to. How could we deny her something like that? In the long run it would probably hurt her. She would realize no fairytale dad was going to come. I wanted her to be able to make the choice. I didn't want to crush her hopes with her dad. The thing is though, there is a huge difference between a father and a dad. So how do you explain that to a fragile ten year old girl?

Neither Gabriel nor I wanted to go with Dad. The only problem was that it just wasn't right for her to go with him alone. We would not let that happen, especially when our mom worried about it too. I wasn't risking anything.

"If we just didn't see him anymore, it would be so much easier." His words sounded like a plea. I hated to see him like this. Over something I couldn't fix.

"I told you, I'll go with Anna by myself if you don't want to anymore." I had told Gabriel before that I was willing to. He always gave and sacrificed so much for us. I wanted to give something back. As usual, he declined.

"No, I wouldn't feel right. Nothing to do here anyway." He said.

Our mom walked into the doorway of the room.

"Your dad is waiting outside for you." She said.

Yay. Not. We walked outside to leave. Gabriel paused next to Mom. He apologized for acting up earlier. She wrapped him in a hug. Then we climbed into his truck, waved goodbye, and drove off.

"Where are we going?" Anna asked eagerly.

Gabriel sat silently in the front seat watching out the window as Dad answered Anna's question.

"It's Lilly's birthday." Lilly was just another neglected child my father just so happened to produce. She was still young. "She turned three last week and today is her party."

I was tempted to ask what day of last week her birthday was. I doubt he would've known. It wasn't worth starting a fight already. Was his enthusiasm fake for Anna? How could he care about another child when he already had three of them that he barely ever talked to or saw?

I saw Gabriel's face reflected back at me from the side view mirror. From one look I could tell his thoughts matched my own. The only difference was that his were more explicit. I sent him a text message.

R u ok?

His reply is longer than expected since I was already surprised he had answered me in the first place.

O I'm gr8. Do u think he'd be upset if I jumped out of the car?

I glared at him. I hope that he caught the look. He shouldn't be thinking like that. It wasn't worth letting Dad get to him that way.

I don't know if he would care. I would, and Anna would.

I received no reply. I was only calmed by the knowledge that I knew Gabriel didn't have it in him to hurt himself. Often, he said it would be better if he was gone. I didn't like the comment. It scared me, quite frankly. I asked him what he'd meant by that. He told me he didn't mean death. Mostly he just wanted to leave. Be away from the pain that he felt trapped in. Running away had been an option he considered. Later he abandoned the idea because he felt he wouldn't make it, not while knowing what he would have left behind for his two sisters to handle alone. Now he just wanted to move into our grandparent's house.

The rest of the ride was filled with chatter from Dad and Anna. We pulled up to a trailer. The back yard was fenced in and a small party was being held. Dad was already out of the truck. He handed Anna a present for us to give to the baby. I don't really know if you would consider her a baby anymore. Slowly, Gabriel and I got out of the truck.

It may have been rude to be this open about not wanting to be here. At this point, I didn't really care. I froze when Dad put an arm around his son, pulling him into a deformed hug.

"How's my favorite son?" If there was a knife present would Gabe had put it through his back?

His eyes looked like liquid fire. It was like coming in contact with a poisonous snake. You didn't want to move too fast. I wasn't sure which one the snake was at the moment.

"I'm your only son, I doubt I'm your favorite anything. I can be your least favorite son. Wouldn't have surprised me." Gabriel's words were thick with anger. Shrugging out of the hug he walked briskly to the home.

"How have you been Baby!" Heather squealed as she wrapped her arms around Dad.

I think I almost puked. I didn't hate this woman. I didn't know her well enough to hate her. I didn't like her though. I just wasn't fond of the cheesy smile. The eyes that screamed do not trust. Maybe I wasn't being fair. All the mistrust and resentment could've come from her boyfriend.

In my mind, it was bad enough that he did nothing for three kids. Did there really have to be a fourth? Apparently there had to be five. One look at Heather's swollen belly informed me of that. She was pregnant, again. With another from my dad? Where does God come in and say enough?

One day I was ranting about my father and questioned out loud how many children he had. Were there any others? Any other poor children that would never see him? If they never met him, he might actually be doing them a favor.

We walked into the yard to join the party. There were lots of younger kids that were Lilly's age. There were a few older ones, close to my age, as well. I could tell Gabriel wanted to leave. Instead he walked over to a table and got something to eat.

I watched him carefully. Gabriel didn't deserve all of this. It had to be torture to him. Then again, did any of us deserve it? Did any one of us not look at it like a form of punishment? I never thought we had done something to deserve this. One of us had to have screwed up somewhere along the line. How else could this be justified?

Heather's son came over to me. He offered me something to drink. I took it. I thought about eating to. I was debating whether or not food would settle me or make me sick.

Nathan was a good kid, I guess. He was always very quiet. I think he was abused as a child but never asked. He turned and I caught sight of a black eye. He was shy, but in a way that made you feel like he felt threatened by anyone standing too close.

"What happened?" He didn't have to ask what I was talking about. He already had seen me staring.

"Got into a nasty fight, you should see the other guy," I was awarded a fake serious face. Nathan wasn't a fighter. I had only known him for a short period of time, but knew this was his attempt at humor. He usually kept to the background; which is why I didn't notice him when I came in.

I didn't feel a huge connection towards Nathan. He was not a brother, and not quite

21

a friend. Maybe because I was so used to the kind of bond Gabriel and I shared, or the protective instinct I had developed towards Anna. Nathan spurred nothing like that inside of me. Perhaps pity, or understanding were words that would fit.

At the moment, Anna was entertaining herself with Lilly. Consuming her time with trying to force the child to play with a ball. Lilly ignored the attempts and showed her preference for the blocks. Anna gave up and gave in. Her new struggle was to have Lilly build a tower instead of breaking them. It was comical to watch them together.

Anna was like a guard dog for Lilly. She didn't want anyone around Lilly. It was like she owned her. She was finally older. She could pass along knowledge now.

Soon I noticed Nathan and Gabriel with a couple of girls my age. I decided to go over. I guess I could be somewhat social while I was here. I made my way over and was greeted by dramatic smiles and highlighted eyes. Not my exact group of people, but I needed someone to talk to. I asked them if they knew Heather well. It turned out that two of the girls were her nieces. The other two were their friends.

The rest of the party passed in a blur. I tried to keep a conversation with the girls at first. Then I felt as if just talking to them made me tired. I went over to a swing and sat with Gabriel instead. It was getting dark, and I was barely paying attention to the words that flowed between Gabriel and Nathan every few minutes.

My brother and I were still thankful when it was time to go home. Gabriel went over and picked up a sleeping Anna. He was careful with her, trying to make sure he didn't wake her up. Sometimes it surprised me to see Gabriel being the one to do these things instead of her own father. He kept trying to take the role.

The drive home was quiet. I watched out the window and saw the soothing colors of fall. Closing my eyes I was close to drifting asleep. I snapped awake, I couldn't fall asleep. I felt vulnerable. Nothing felt safe. Then my phone vibrated. It was from

Gabriel. I looked up towards him and saw he was tense.

I want to yell at him.

What was there to yell at him for? Not talking to us at the party? Using a ten year old as a babysitter so he didn't have to play with his youngest child? I went to ask him but I was too late. I was going to find out.

"So Dad," Gabriel began, anger lingered on every word. "You really haven't talked to me or Hope today." I hadn't really noticed that nothing had been said to me. Most of the time I preferred it that way. It wasn't a shocker when Gabriel pointed it out though.

"I'm sorry. I thought you were busy making friends." Oh and the lies begin. His voice raises because he is trying to defend himself with false reasons. Who was here that he had to pretend for now?

"No, you never talk to me anymore, or Hope. You can't look at us without recoiling. It's like we make you sick. You can't even look at me in the eye."

"Hope you know I love you. You know I love both of you." He tried this tactic often. The "please you know it isn't that way" tone. Did he realize it made my stomach turn?

"No, I don't know that. I hate to admit it because I don't want it to be true, but you never even make an attempt to show me you care anymore. I've ruled out you loving me as an option. Toleration maybe." My words were as cold as Gabriel's. I looked down at Anna. I was happy to find that she was still asleep and didn't have to listen to our fight.

Gabriel had a pleased look on his face. He was happy that I had backed him up. Even if he already knew what I felt, he liked when I spoke out like this about it. He was glad that I was becoming more vocal. Less restraint now would be better than later when we were home. So why not let it out when the opportunity arose?

He stared at our dad the rest of the way, but he didn't speak about it anymore. He was absolutely quiet the whole way home. This was why we didn't talk to him about what we felt. He wouldn't listen. He would start to defend himself, and then knowing he would lose the argument he gave up.

"Typical," I spit through clenched teeth. I didn't get my chance to vent. At least Gabriel got some of the words out.

Anna woke up just before we entered our driveway. We climbed out of the truck and found our mom waiting for us on the porch. Dad greeted her and she acknowledged him with a small nod. He explained where he had taken us. Acting all excited as he spoke about Lilly. It didn't look like she was in the mood to talk to him. I sidestepped a hug after passing him. I was done with him. We told him goodbye and walked to the porch to stand by Mom.

The closer I got to her the more upset she seemed to look. Had she had a fight with her boyfriend? It angered me that in many ways he was alike to my own dad. He would drink for the pleasure of it, or he would crave it and drink heavily. I couldn't stand it. It made me sick. Could he truly not tell how repulsive it was to the rest of us?

Gabriel and I had promised each other we would never drink. It wasn't like we needed the promise. But it felt good to say it out loud. Anna promised too. She was glad to be part of something.

My mother's boyfriend was always fine when he was drinking at a party or out around friends. It was when he came home that he was a problem. He would be violent or rude. It wasn't the violence that worried me. He never hit my mother, thank God. His rage was more directed at inanimate objects. The fact that I saw bits and pieces of the man my father was scared me.

At least he wasn't as bad as my dad. Many times I had gone into the basement and gagged because of the filthy smell that lingered in the air. The one room turned into his crypt. I would find my dad in this room. He would be passed out in a chair or on the couch that he stowed away down there. Bottles and cans would litter the area around him.

How much could he drink before it just killed him? Was he trying to end his life with the foul substance? It was his only form of comfort now. What he turned to when he was saddened or in pain. He is wasting away. I can see it whenever I look in his eyes.

Chapter 2

I help Gabriel get Anna into the house. Dad has already driven away. There is no need for him to stay any longer. He's done his part for the night. Mom steps closer and takes Anna out of Gabriel's arms. She kisses us both on the head and asks if we had a good time. Then she asks if we're still hungry.

"No, we ate enough at the party I think." I tell her.

I go to take a shower to wash the day off of my skin. The warm water calms my frayed nerves. I thought about everything Gabriel said in the car. I think about his message. How he had the desire to yell at our dad. I know he feels stressed. We always do around him. I gave up yelling. It doesn't help, he doesn't listen to a word that is said anyway. If something you say phases him, don't expect the feeling to last long. As soon as he gets home he drinks all of his pain away.

Alcohol is killing him slowly. Day by day, it wears down on him. This only causes him to drink more than he does. After watching the beer age my dad over the years, I became sick at the sight or smell of his escape. I knew Anna wouldn't try it, but I was worried Gabriel would.

He would use it like my dad did. As a safety net. Something to hold him up when he was in pain. I didn't want to see him that way. I didn't want to watch him become the shell of a person that he could be. It didn't seem to appeal to Gabriel, and he didn't seem to have any trouble staying away from it. He used music to calm himself. I will always be proud of my brother's strength.

I'm dreaming, I have to be. Those sounds I hear couldn't really be happening. Oh God no, please no, not again. Another one of my mother's piercing screams fills the air. The dog is going nuts. I hear Shadow slam against the door over and over. He just keeps barking.

I turn and find myself looking at a younger version of Gabriel, I'm begging him to stay with Anna and me. We are curled up on the bed crying. My brother's dirty blond hair sticks up from his head in tufts. Anna is buried in my shirt crying louder than the rest of us. More screams. Gabriel lurches out of bed.

"No!" This scream belongs to me.

I grasp his arm, and pull him against me. He gets back up; his eyes are red from crying so hard.

"I am not leaving her out there!" He screams back at me. Then he breaks down. He pulls me onto the bed. Anna howls into his side. I hear the door break open.

I hit the floor hard as I tumble out of my bed. I hate feeling trapped. In that dream, I feel like there is no escape from the horror. No, not a dream. I hate nightmares. Especially the ones where you know it's not real but you just can't get out of it. Do you know what's even more terrible? When your "nightmare" is a memory. I felt like I was there. The mood, the sounds, and the feelings were all the same. You get so caught up in nightmares when they turn out to be the past. An old reality that you've gone through.

I roll over so I can see my clock. It is just after one. I get up, fix my sheets and climb back into bed. Will this be another sleepless night? I can't let it be. I have tests to take in the morning. I need sleep. I need to at least rest. Where is Shadow when you need him?

I must have dozed off on my own because the next thing I know my mom is begging me to wake up and get dressed for the day. I'm groggy, but don't feel like being late today. I head outside after I'm ready and meet Gabriel and a handful of other kids from the street who are ready for the day.

I notice one girl, Nicole, who is blatantly admiring Gabriel. I've only talked to her once. I regret it, too. The whole time she went on about how lucky I was to have Gabriel in my house. That it was a curse for him to be my brother. I choked on what I had been eating. She didn't even care to notice and continued.

"He really is an angel isn't he? It's too bad I don't see him more often during school. Don't you think his eyes are amazing?" Gabriel had gray eyes like our dad. He hated them because of it.

I stared at the girl and tried to figure out what Gabriel had ever said to her to cause the hero worship that she had for him. I tried to block out the rest of the conversation about how lovely his hair was.

No one really looked much like our dad besides Gabriel. Not even Lilly possessed the characteristics he had. Both of the men shared the dirty blond hair and gray eyes. They shared the same long lean build, as well. One difference was that Gabriel had worked hard for an athlete's body, there Dad fell short. He looked like a drunk. Heavier set and lazy.

Gabriel had long lean muscles. He worked out often and it showed. Once he told me that the physical exercise calmed him. He told me I should try it. That it might help me. So I took up running. Of course, now every time my blood boils, I want to do laps instead of punching someone, but beggars can't be choosers.

Anna and I share our mother's traits. Hazel eyes and long straight hair with natural golden streaks. I never questioned if Gabe would have rather looked like our mom or not. I'm sure he would. There never was a point to asking. The part that made me wonder was that I had assumed Gabriel looked at himself as someone our dad could have been. Although, he doesn't like being compared to Dad though.

The bus pulls up and we board, looking for our seats. I pick the one where my best friend sits. Rachel scoots her things to the side making room for me to sit down beside her. She had been such a good friend to me for so long, and I trusted her opinion more than my own on many occasions.

She has black hair that fell to her shoulders. Some days she would add red or blue streaks to her hair. She was funny and nice to just about everyone. She didn't like to think so, but she really was a special and beautiful girl. She had helped me through a lot of hard days when I didn't want to be around anyone but her. My best friend. If I could have adopted her as my sister, I would have in a heart beat. She made a wonderful artist, and when she painted, I watched how her hand moved and created the scene in her head.

We were involved with a lot of the same things in school, and many of our classes fell together at the same time. Today, for instance, we would have gym together after homeroom. At the moment there was nothing I'd rather do than go let out some energy.

I met Rachel by her locker, and we headed to the locker room to get changed for class. Our gym was mixed with anything from freshman to seniors. Gabriel just happened to be assigned to our class for the year.

He enjoyed this. He had liked Rachel for two years now. He had always thought she was pretty, now he thought she was old enough that he might have a chance. During gym he would try to impress her by showing off. He didn't ignore me. Usually he tried to show me up. He had some competition. We were both athletic and fast.

We were playing dodge ball today, and I saw Gabriel grin wickedly towards me out of the corner of my eye. He was going to have too much fun with this. He won many of the games, and Rachel looked impressed. Especially when it came down to the two of them and he cornered her. If he ever got her with the ball, it was a light tap. We use soft foam balls, but he still manages to leave welts on me.

The relaxing time is interrupted by an announcement from the school office. Gabriel and I are called down. Rachel looks confused. We couldn't be in trouble since both of us have been called. I'm quick to panic when I all but sprint out of the room. I don't care if people look at me funny. Right now, all I care about is if my little sister and mother are alright. If they are safe and well.

I would rather be in trouble than have something happen to one of them.

Gabriel catches me and slows me down. He is worried too, only he isn't panicking the way I am at the moment. It calms me a bit to see that he isn't overly worried.

I walk into the office and find my mother and sister there. They are safe. My whole body relaxes. I don't know why I thought they hadn't been okay. Guess I'm just used to bad surprises.

Now I was curious. If no one was hurt, then what was wrong? I saw my mom's face for the first time. She had been crying.

"Shadow is dying," she said, her body started to tremble. "I can't watch it anymore."

Our dog was sick? He had been fine when I left for school this morning! However, I knew it was true though. For the past couple of months he had been slowing down. Growing old in a fast forward rate. He wasn't ready to go though. Not when we still needed him so much. He was staying for us.

"Is he sick?" Gabriel asked.

"He's just old. He won't drink or move. I tried to get food and water into him but it only made things worse."

Impossible, I thought, as we walked through the school parking lot. He couldn't be this bad this soon. I looked over at my mom. She was trying to hide that she wanted to cry. By the time we reached the car, she was sobbing. It wouldn't be good for her to drive this way. I wasn't the only one who noticed. Gabriel took the keys and drove us home.

Mom was crying so hard. She loved that dog. We all loved Shadow. He was family. Shadow was special. He couldn't just die. I felt like there wasn't anyway he could be gone.

"I wanted you kids to see him one last time before he died." Mom said in between choked sobs.

Memories passed through my mind. Playing fetch with him. Picking him out of the rest of the puppies. Carrying him home on my lap. Gabriel and me fighting over a name for him. Anna riding him like a horse when she was little. Then I shut out the next string of memories. The screams, the shrieks, the pleas for help. I didn't want to think about it right now. I couldn't lose Shadow. I couldn't lose something that meant so much to me.

We got home and ran into the house. We found Shadow. He was moving around and coming to see us.

"I thought you said he was dying!" I said to our mom. I was furious, Shadow dying was not a joking matter. Mom looked surprised. She explained Shadow was sick that he would in fact die. Gabriel looked at him. He bent down and stroked his best friend behind the ear.

"It's his second wind." He said. I knew what that meant, our pet was slowly dying away. Our guardian angel was trying to stay, but his attempts would be in vain. He wouldn't make it.

I looked at his face. I finally noticed how old he really looked. I spotted the gray hairs that speckled his fur. I didn't like what

I saw. Mom called the vet and scheduled an appointment to put him down tomorrow. Too soon, I thought. I didn't want him to suffer.

I didn't sleep well that night. I went in the living room and sat in a chair. I watched Shadow. I wouldn't get to spend anymore time with him than now. He wouldn't be there for me anymore sleepless nights. I sighed, I had to say goodbye at some point. It just wasn't easy to say goodbye.

I felt a hand lay on my shoulder and jumped. When I turned, I saw a dark figure and went to scream. A large hand covered my mouth, muffling the sound. I bit down hard on one of the fingers til I tasted blood. Shadow growled lightly. A warning for us to keep it down. Gabriel winced. I punched him hard, and felt the breath leave his lungs.

"What was that for," he gasped.

"You gave me a heart attack!" I growled back.

"Sorry, I just wanted to talk about Shadow. I was on my way to your room, but noticed you were in here." He waited for an answer.

"What can I say? He's dying."

"That's not what I mean." Gabriel said.

"What then?"

"Do you think mom is too willing to give him up?" He paused. "Not that any of us could. I guess I just feel like I don't know if she wants him down or not."

"Of course she doesn't want to," I said "you know that. She's stuck between helping him and hurting all of us."

He sighed. No one could ever understand the importance of our dog. Gabriel and I sat there and remembered.

It had been a long day. We were laying in bed together with our mom. Gabriel was 9, I was 7, and Anna was 3. Our parents had been fighting that day. Dad had left afterwards. We were waiting for him to come back. It was late.

Mom heard him pull in and went down to talk to him. There was a few minutes and then some yelling started. It upset us to hear it again so soon. I was worried, I always hated fighting. Then we heard it, the first of many agonizing screams filled the air. Her pleas, begging for someone, anyone to come help her. Why wouldn't someone go help her? There were neighbors, I knew they heard it as well. It was loud. How could they just ignore it?

We listened, crying, as she begged for him to stop. Shadow barked and growled. He wanted out of the house. He barked and lunged at the door repeatedly. We still remained safe upstairs in her bed.

Wanting to be brave, Gabriel started to climb out of bed.

"Where are you going?" I asked.

"To help, someone has to help her."

"I'm coming too then."

Anna crawled over crying, "Don't go sissy no. Don't go."

"Gabe," I said with tears in my eyes, "We can't leave her Gabe."

"Stay here with her then." He hollered.

He was crying hard now. Scared to death, but wanting to be brave and help. There wouldn't have been anything he could've done to stop it. He had to have known he couldn't save her. He wanted to try though. Someone needed to try.

Gabriel was too worked up to even think straight, I convinced him to get back in bed. I was worried for him. I was worried for my mother. Her cries continued. She cried out for him to stop. She screamed in agony.

I heard the door slam against the wall. No one came in, the noises outside continued. A new sound filled outside. Shadow had opened the door. He was outside. We listened as Shadow tackled our dad to the ground. I heard my poor beaten mother sob loudly.

Somehow she was able to climb up the porch steps and get into the door. She called for Shadow to come, he continued to snarl and growl, but made his way to her. Once inside she locked the door. My siblings and I cried, we were so scared. Even though we knew it was our mom, we shook and huddled together. Holding one another for some sense of security.

She drug herself into the room. We cried for her. She shut and locked her bedroom door. Shadow paced around the room with the fur still standing up on his back. She managed to get into the bed and collapsed. She sobbed into the pillow. We tried to help her under the covers and cried with her. Too scared to speak or ask what had happened. We fell asleep that night clinging to her. Shadow guarding us from any harm.

In the morning we knew she was hurt. She had a hard time getting up and moving. She was taken to a doctor, and we stayed with our grandparents. Later, we learned that her neck had been broken in several spots during the night.

This is the night that haunts my nightmares. The memory that took my bright world, and drug it threw the dark, staining it permanently. There was no going back. I would never forget. There would never be a time that I would be able to look back on that night and not feel ripped up inside.

How could any sort of a man lay a hand on a woman, let alone beat her? How could he raise his hand up against her and strike her down? What kind of person did that to one they loved? I can't answer if he was drunk or not. Even if he was, that wouldn't be an excuse. There is no excuse for what he did. There never could be an excuse, or a reason to justify what he did.

To top off the misery? He never went to jail. This was a crime. Why didn't the judge find him guilty? He had a good attorney. Doesn't that show justice? A good attorney, and you'll win your case. What kind of judge would not listen to a x-ray? There was a story for that as well. I guess she was never hit by him. She just happened to fall down the front porch stairs.

I do not see how he was allowed to skate free after what he did. The pain of it never goes away. The memory will always be burned into our minds, but he won't have to deal with the pain.

I never talked to my dad about what happened that night. I'm sure Gabriel or I could've at some point. There was fear in even mentioning that night. We could've confronted him. What do you say to a man who tried to murder your own mother? What do you say to that man when he turns out to be your dad? The very man she thought loved her, and she loved in return?

I look up at Gabriel. His eyes are red also. He holds back tears. We both already cried. What was the point in crying? It just felt better to let it all out. Even if it happened years ago, the pain from something like that never subsides. Especially when you have no closure. It would probably have been easier if he had just gone to jail.

No, the pain never would diminish. Instead God gave us the strength to live with it each and every day of our lives. He kept my mom alive. He gave us hope in that. How can I not believe that he will give me the strength and determination I need to make it through everything I will have to face?

"Do you think he would've actually killed her?" I ask Gabriel, my throat thick with tears.

"If he tried, and came that close to it, I don't see what would've stopped him. Besides Shadow that is." At the sound of his name Shadow looked up.

"Do you think he would've killed us too?" I start crying again quietly. I never admitted it to Gabriel, but I always knew we could've died that night just as easily.

"Maybe, I don't know what would've stopped him. He probably would've." Gabriel said wiping his eyes.

"Do you think he cares?"

"If he cared, don't you think he'd say something? Don't you think he'd talk to us instead of acting like it never happened?" Gabriel said. "Instead he sits at home and drinks away any fear or pain. I hate how weak he is."

"I believe that," I didn't have to believe, I knew it was true. "Do you think if maybe we talked to him about it, things would be better?"

"How?" Gabriel asked, looking at me like I was crazy. Like I should know better than to even think or say that. But light touched his eyes. Anything that would wake up our father, any chance, just made things easier to handle.

"I don't really know." I admit.

"What would it prove? It wouldn't go away. It can't be undone. He's waited too long to make things any better." Fresh tears spill from Gabriel's eyes. "What would it do for us Hope?"

"I just want an apology. I know he can't give that and mean it. I know it wouldn't make things better. I just want him to take responsibility for what he did to us." Is that really all I wanted? For him to admit it? In truth, it would be a long shot for it to even happen. At least it would be an end to the knowledge that he never was punished. This could be his punishment. He would have to be willing to give it to himself. He would have to take responsibility for his actions. If not in front of the world, at least to his children. He owed us that much.

He punishes himself as it is. By drinking, he's killing his body. Making it worthless. Giving it no hope. At least, if he admitted it, we would have some closure. Isn't something better than nothing?

Chapter 3

"Do you think it affected us a lot?" Gabriel asks me.

"I don't see how it couldn't have, but when I look at us, I don't see how it did."

He nods, but we feel the same way. It's not the answer either of us are looking for. We want to know how we were affected. How we were changed. I'm sure we could find out if we really watched, but I can't bare to pick myself apart that way.

"How do you think it affected me?" Gabriel was terrified that he would end up like our father. He told me once he wasn't sure if he wanted to have kids, because he didn't want them to go through anything remotely close to what we had. Through the night I reassured him that he was nothing like our father. He never had been, nor would he ever be. I would never let him turn into something like that. Besides, Gabriel was strong. He would never be the weak person Dad was.

When the sun started to rise, I laughed lightly. I wanted to take the edge off of the night. We would be going through enough as it was today.

"Look at us," I said. "Aren't we great siblings. We get along better than most. We sit up through the night and actually help one another."

Shadow had stayed with us during the night. Gabriel reached down and scratched behind his ear. Then he picked up a pillow and laid down next to the dog. I followed his example, but used Shadow as my pillow. When we woke up in the morning, our dear friend was gone. His body was all that was left.

Our mom cried and spent most of the day in her room. When Anna woke up she searched for him all over the house. Soon she realized what had happened through the night. She came over to me and cried. We all cried together. When the sound reached our mother's room, she came out to see us. We held on to each other for half an hour just letting everything out. We all felt the loss of our Shadow. We already missed him.

He was buried that day. Now he lays under an apple tree in the yard. We picked this spot because he loved the tree. He thought the apples were toys for him to play with. We would play for hours. Every time an apple was thrown, he would retrieve it.

At the end of the night we sat in the kitchen, I was holding my mom close.

"Hope?" She whispered.

"Yeah mom?" I wondered what it was, I didn't want to see anymore tears today. I had cried myself out.

"I want you to know how proud I am of you, of all of you. I want you three to know how much you mean to me and how much I love you." She looked at each one of us as she said this.

I truly loved my mom. We all told her we loved her back. Wrapping up the family with a big sappy group hug. Her boyfriend even came in to join us. Usually he shied away from any kind of family bonding like this. Tonight, he could tell our mom needed it.

We brought up happy memories to share with each other about Shadow. We didn't bring up that he had saved our mother's life, and possibly all of our own as well. We wanted to say something about it, just to get it out there.

I was grateful to have someone here for my mom. He helped with burying Shadow. At least he cared if she was somewhat happy. It was a bonus on his part. Something my dad would never have done.

We still had to go to school. No one wanted to, but there really wasn't a good enough excuse that the school would let all of us stay home. Mom drove us since we got up late and missed the bus. Rachel found me as soon as I walked through the door on Wednesday morning.

I told her what had happened last night. I told her how I had woken up to find myself laying on him. At least he died at home with us, rather than having to go to the vet. Rachel comforted me throughout the day.

She knew what Shadow had done. She knew how much he meant to us.

Rachel had been one of the few people I sat down and cried to about everything that happened. I always felt like it was a violation to tell someone about it. It didn't seem like my story to share. It seemed more like it was my mother's story. Over the years, I came to see it was mine, too. I had gone through it. I had changed as a result of it. I felt the need to get it of my chest. To go out and let people know what happened. So I started telling my friends.

You know the song about finding out who your true friends are? I found mine. They were the ones I could trust to listen. I felt guilty for it, but I was glad not to have to keep it in any longer.

Most of them were shocked and surprised. They hadn't known my parents were divorced, let alone that my mother had been abused. I didn't want pitied and was worried that was all I would receive from my friends as forms of support. I was happy when I wasn't looked at like a victim. I was happy when my friends saw me and saw my strength. Not only mine, but my family's strength as well.

Yes, it is my story. I lived it and am still living it to this day. And I will never look in the mirror and shun myself. I will always be able to look in the eyes of the person looking back at me. If I can do this, I know I will make it through and be the person I was meant to be. Not someone affected by tragedy, but someone who overcame it.

I want everyone to see Gabriel and see how calm he is able to be even with his temper. I want people to look at Anna and see what a brave and strong little girl she is. I want them to see how happy she always is. What do I want people to see when they looked at me? Probably the strength. A person who had gone through so much, continued to, and still didn't break under the pressure of it all. If anyone judges me or my family, I at least want them to know what we went through first. We have stayed strong throughout the years.

I learned something. Everyone is affected by their own situations differently. We all go through something, what defines us as ourselves in our eyes. What it has turned us into as people. We all undertake something different. It shapes each and everyone of us.

Our experience gave Gabriel a short fuse with people who didn't deserve patience. It made me grow up fast. It left Anna lost and confused often. She kept looking for a father, or at least a father figure. She looked for one in our mom's boyfriend. Most of the time she was disappointed in what she found. I thought that she was too young to realize the reason behind it. Gabriel and I knew.

For years we always said we lost our dad. That he wasn't here anymore. We know that just wasn't the case. We didn't know what a dad should be to his family because we never had that before. We never had a dad to lose. So we didn't lose him. He didn't go away. He just wasn't there in the first place.

I told Rachel all of this. I told Gabriel all of this. Only recently I started telling my mom. I never wanted her to worry about me or how I was taking things. I didn't want her to think that I couldn't handle things or that I needed some kind of therapy. I could handle all of this in one way or another. If I couldn't, God wouldn't have burdened me with it in the first place. If God knew I was strong enough, then I knew that too.

○●○

Today seemed to keep getting worse. Not only for me, but Gabriel as well. He had gotten into a fight with a boy who had mocked him for being upset over Shadow. Gabriel won the fight. He left the fight with what would turn into a bruise or two. The other guy, most likely, had a broken nose. His lip was busted, and the rest of his face looked like a mess.

Gabriel was in fights before. Most of the time he just pinned the other guy. Never did he punch or cause someone to bleed. He usually was calm and wasn't aggressive. Lately he was getting more aggressive. I didn't like it. Maybe he was still just upset from Shadow. I really hoped so.

He will probably have to talk with the counselor over the conflict. He would hate it. I understood since I had similar feelings towards the subject. Since he had been forced to talk to someone about the incident with our dad he hated talking to other people about his feelings and thoughts. Unless it was me. He was fine when it was just the two of us venting about things. I was glad I could at least help him with that. He thought that anyone else he talked to wouldn't be doing it to help him, but because it was their job.

As much as we denied it, we probably would benefit from talking to someone about everything. I needed closure. There wasn't any. I used to agree with Gabriel, I thought revenge was in order. After all, he hadn't gone to jail. Even though he should have. Gabriel also thought that the best form of this revenge would be for Dad to have a taste of what he dished out. What Gabriel meant by this, was that he wanted someone to go and beat our dad. To break him so he knew how I felt. I made him stop thinking that way. Even if I had wanted it, too, at one time.

I told him that if we did anything in retaliation, or had someone else do it, then we would be no better than he was. Just because he had to resort to abuse, didn't mean we had to. I thought Gabriel was going to hit me. He calmed himself quickly and left the room.

Mom wasn't happy when she had to take him out of school early. He would be suspended for three days. He said he didn't care. To him it made no difference. He would get the work done and there would be nothing to worry about.

Teachers were usually puzzled when Gabriel was in trouble. He was always a good student. He excelled in the classroom and during sports. Sometimes he just let his temper get the best of him. It was hard to get that kind of physical reaction out of him. Usually, he shrugged things off. I hoped the only reason he was acting like this was because of Shadow.

Chapter 4

"Gabriel you are grounded! You will be doing chores all week. You will work until your hands bleed, and you pass out at the end of the night!"

I wish she'd stop screaming. I look over at Hope. I raise my eyebrows at her. She looks like she's about ready to cry.

It's my fault. I accepted that. I got into the fight. I beat up the punk. Now, I am putting my family through more because of my stupidity. How is that fair?

"Isn't there a child labor law in place so that doesn't happen?" I ask. It probably comes out sounding snobby though. Hope hides a smile. I am glad that I could bring one out of her. She was a pretty good actor. Always good at hiding her thoughts and feelings. I was the opposite. I let what I felt be known. I was only good at being calm, even when I was angry.

Yes I stayed calm. I didn't go out on a blind rage. Instead, I sat there slowly burning through my emotions. I would go through each emotion completely, letting it bleed it's way out of me. This was how I sat there and stayed calm.

That wasn't true today. I can't believe I punched that punk so hard. He shouldn't have even started with me. I was having a bad enough week as it was.

"Here is a list of things you have to do while your suspended. I don't know what all you'll be doing afterwards yet. I can't believe you. Starting fights, and at the beginning of the year no less."

I took the list from her. It was long. Full of things like cutting the grass, doing the laundry, and picking Anna up after school. I didn't have my own car yet and would have to walk. It was only a mile there and back. There was a bus that could take her home, but she wanted to be home in time for dinner. If she took the bus, that wouldn't happen. I couldn't be made to cut the grass for long since it was getting closer to winter.

"Also you need to call your dad and tell him what happened today." She said. This wasn't punishment. That could only be described as torture in itself.

Hope's eyes got wide. She knew how badly I hated calling him. How badly I hated showing any attempt at building a relationship with him. Communication between us was not something I wanted.

Sometimes I even had trouble yelling at him. I knew he didn't care what I had to say. Why keep up a pretense? I knew I had to call though, and there would be no way around it.

I picked up my phone. The sooner this was taken care of the better. There was a new message from Hope

Breathe

I hadn't even noticed that she had sent it. I forced my fingers to dial that horrid number. I would much rather forget about it. Pretend nothing had gone wrong today. Then I took a deep breath and hit send. He answered right before it was able to go to voice mail.

"Hello?" A cheery voice greeted me. How could he be cheery?

"I was told to call and tell you I got suspended today." I told him. I could picture him smiling at the other end of the line. Like me being violent made him happy.

"Did you win?"

Wasn't this the sort of conversation a dad and his son were supposed to have? A boy's mom would be all mad, and the dad pretends to sit him down and read him the riot act, when all he is really doing is commending him. Then I realized I wasn't talking to a dad. I wasn't even talking to a friend. On the other end was a would be murderer.

I'm pretty sure the blood in my veins turned into ice water.

"Yeah, I won. I got suspended for three days." My voice was dry. Lacking any energy needed to keep up a real conversation.

He laughed at that, or was it at me?

"Don't tell your mom, but congrats," He said.

Again, the sick feeling returned. It ate its way through me and landed in my stomach. Proud of me winning. Proud of me hurting someone. Defense was one thing, violence was another. Couldn't he see the difference? Apparently, that was asking for too much.

A thought went through my head, "that's how father-son relationships work." Was our relationship that? I almost laughed at myself for questioning it. It never had been and never would be. At one point in my life, I thought we had it. I remember the day I found out we didn't.

I had been trying to teach myself to ride a skateboard. I got stupid and went inside to practice on the kitchen floor. Of course, it was an epic failure. I broke my arm when I landed on the tile floor. My dad never helped me. He never tried to help me get up. When I asked to go to the hospital, he told me I didn't need to.

My mom ended up taking me to the hospital. My arm was broken in more than one spot. When we got home that night,

Dad was sleeping on the couch. I kept asking for help to get into the house, because everyone else was still down at the car. I yelled to try to wake him up. Nothing worked. I ended up getting frustrated. My hands were full, and I was in a cast. It wouldn't be easy to get back in the house.

Needless to say, I tried. When I finally managed the door and walked in, it caught my ankle. I fell hard on the ground. I landed on my newly broken arm and howled in pain. Everyone came running to help, except my dad, who rolled back over so he could get some sleep. I didn't want to go back to the hospital. I told my mom I was fine. After a while, she said alright.

My "Dad" had left me on the floor. He didn't give me a second thought. It hadn't even phased him. Me being in pain wasn't enough to get him to move.

I noticed then that Dad was still talking.

"Don't forget, I'll see you sometime this weekend. I'll call and let you know if I'm working or not." The call disconnected.

I wanted to throw my phone. I went and found Mom.

"I don't want to go with him anymore." I said.

"I know, I'm sorry. Tell him that. I can't just send your sisters alone though." She knew she had me there. I refused to let them be alone with him. I promised not to let it happen. I didn't want anyone with him.

"How does it make sense that he can neglect and ignore us for months, but as soon as he decides he wants to see us and act like he's part of our lives, he gets to? Where does that make sense? It's like letting him snap his fingers and say he's a good parent."

"Why are you telling me all of this now?" She wasn't mad when she said this. She was curious. To her, it looked like we had been getting along better, but things never really changed. Instead, I tried harder than ever to distance myself from him. I'm sure he noticed this, but he never pointed it out.

Hope walked in and interrupted our talk. She looked back and forth between us. Once she was confident that it was no longer a fight, she left the room.

"I won't force you to go with him." she said.

"I'll deal with it," I had before, so I knew I could now. "It's better for Hope and Anna if I do anyway."

"How so?"

"So they still have the option to decide if they want a dad." I told her.

"Do you really think that is worth it?"

"Not really." I hated admitting it to her, but she needed to hear it. We both already knew it was true anyways. "He was never there for us, or you. A majority of the time he came home he was drunk."

"He just doesn't know how to be a dad." She wasn't defending him. She said it in a matter of fact kind of way.

"Yeah, well he no longer deserves the title of being our dad!"

"I'm sorry Gabriel, I can't change who he is." It stressed her to talk about this. Especially after I was already in trouble.

"Shouldn't you be in bed?" She asked, obviously done with the matter. I walked away.

Sometimes I felt so alone. I haven't told Hope because I don't want her to think she isn't helping me. Even if I tell her a lot of things, and vent with her, I don't know how she would take this. I was worried she would think I was weak.

I feel like I'm the father figure in the house. I know I'm young, and I know there is Steve, but this is my family. I try to be calm and strong for them. Then I get stressed and angry. I stare into the bathroom mirror. I see a younger, healthier version of my dad watching me. Physically we are very similar. I hope we aren't mentally. I want no other part of him in me. I'm scared whenever I find those bits and pieces weeded inside who I am.

I tried talking to someone before. I stopped because I felt like I wasn't being helped. I didn't feel like the person I talked to helped me. I didn't feel like they cared.

All of a sudden anger flooded through my body. I run back into my room and close the door. I pick up a knife laying on my dresser. I slash it over and over again at the wall.

These are the few times I lose my temper this way. I've broken. I feel as if I'm far beyond repair. I drop the knife and stand there shaking violently. I try to calm myself and take deep breaths. I'm only slightly trembling now. I have to get this under control. I can't break like this again.

I'm so tired of the feelings. I don't want him here, and he doesn't want me. I'm never going to be anything to him. He'll never want me. Why does it matter? I've given up on caring.

Chapter 5

I look around the playground. I am looking for Anna. I told Gabriel I would get her today so that he would be able to finish some of the things he needed to do around the house. I finally see her. Is she? Yes, she's sitting at the foot of a slide crying. I run over and ask her what happened. She tells me a whole story about how she was playing and fell and hurt her knee. I examine the scrapes. It had to hurt, but wasn't that bad.

The only reason she was crying was because of the blood. The blood stains across her pale skin. Anna doesn't like being hurt enough to bleed. She could've made the same fall a hundred times over and still been fine. If she had been wearing jeans like she was supposed to be, she wouldn't care.

It's funny how pain works. Sometimes we base it so much off of the physical effects that we forget about the other aspects of it. If you fall and scrape your knee, it isn't the end of the world. On the other hand, if you fall and tear your knee to shreds; you might be a bit more cautious. It's almost like if it's out of sight, it's out of mind.

Absent mindedly I wonder if Anna is scared of pain because of seeing how my mom still hurts from her neck. She is constantly in pain. The old fractures in her neck limit her greatly. I hate to see her hurt from what someone she loved did to her. Sometimes I don't think it's just physical pain that still hurts her, but emotional also.

I'm proud of my mother. No matter what ever happens I always will be. She got through something that would've destroyed other people. She persevered. She made it through. I love to see her strength. Every night I pray I'll be able to be strong like her and Gabriel.

I take Anna home so that I can clean her up. I find the house empty besides Gabriel sitting at the kitchen table doing his make-up work that I brought home for him. I ask

71

him where mom went. He said she went out to the store to pick up milk. Gabriel said that she had told him she would be back shortly.

Good, I felt drained from the day. Outside I walk around the yard and pick the few remaining flowers out of the flower beds. After arranging them into a bouquet, I tie them together with a piece of string. I walk over and lay the small gift on Shadow's grave.

Our mom's boyfriend is getting a gravestone made. It's a surprise for my mom. None of us are supposed to tell her. I'm happy that he is trying to help her through this. I didn't realize how much it actually bothered her. I'd heard her crying and snuck out of my room late at night to see what was wrong. I found her in the kitchen with her boyfriend holding her against him. He was trying to comfort her. Quietly, I crept back into my room so I wouldn't disturb them.

A soft breeze blows. It's already cooling down for the day. Not that it's a good thing

Shadow died, but I'm glad it wasn't in the winter. Having a difficult time burying his body would only make it harder on my mom. She would feel the need to bury him and probably try doing it by herself. She would've hurt herself if she tried. It's not like any part of Shadow could just be thrown away.

I brought my camera outside, and I turn it on. Snapping pictures of the rainbow of leaves on the trees is a good way to relax. I spot a squirrel with a nut diving up into a tree. Luckily, I take the picture before the moment is over. I bring the picture up and look at the frozen moment. Surely Anna will laugh when I show her.

I sit down in the grass and flip through the pictures I've collected. After a while I come across one of my favorites. I had my neighbor take it. I wanted it to be a family picture. Shadow and Anna are in the middle of the shot. Anna is posing on the ground and Shadow stands right above her. Gabe and I are standing off to the right, we are pretending to choke each other. Our mom stands off to the left. She watches us like we are crazy.

I miss times like these. Ones where you know everything is alright. I don't like the days were moments like these are replaced by fights at dinner. It's not often, and I know every family goes through it. Sometimes I just wish we could look at each other and say we got through the worst together and that we'll get through the rest together too.

The things that we try the hardest to escape use the least energy to come back up on us. No one wants to remember those moments. No one wants to only think about fights and arguments, or bad times. We do for some reason though. We want to forget them the most, and then we find ourselves remembering them all the more because of it. Since nobody wants to forget the good moments, we lose them easier. Even if we cling to them. Memories of good times just happen to fade away.

We're all extremely lucky that there is a way to preserve the memories that we want to keep. It's actually very simple. We take pictures. We snap a shot of a sunset, or at a child's birthday party. The things that bring us joy. Anything from a new born baby, to a wave washing up on the beach. It'll be different for everyone too. We all want to remember different moments that made us smile.

$$\bigcirc \bullet \bigcirc$$

When we hear a car pull in, I expect my mother with only milk. Instead I go out to find her with enough food to feed the entire U.S. Army. She must have found good prices. There have been many occasions when she will go out only for a few things, but come back with a trunk full of food.

I show her my picture of the squirrel. She enjoys it, while I enjoy seeing her smile. After we take all the food in, we relax in the living room for the night. I can't help but smile. You can almost breathe in the happiness in the room. I'm scared that the moment will end too soon. Then again, anytime that this ends will be too soon. I want this to be one of those captured moments. Saved forever. I pull my camera out and start snapping dozens of pictures. At first Gabriel looks annoyed. Then I start to make faces at him. He loosens up and comes over to tackle me. He's strong and has me pinned in no time. I fake an injury. He jumps up and starts apologizing rapidly.

My mom watches me, not completely fooled. Gabriel helps me up, and I knock his feet out from under him. He falls hard on the ground. Obviously, he is disappointed in himself for falling for my little trick. Mom is smiling at us. No one is hurt. Anna is sitting on the couch in hysterics.

Anna runs over and jumps on Gabriel before he is able to get back up. Never does she miss this opportunity. Shear joy is evident in her features as he pretends that she is crushing him. What's better for a ten year old than crushing her beast of a brother?

"How about we go to sleep before you break something?" Mom said. She is trying not to laugh herself.

I make a plan to talk to Gabriel before he's asleep tonight. I want to know what all happened during the fight. I want to know what started it and who threw the first punch. I don't want to ruin anyone's mood tonight, though, so maybe it would be best to ask him about it in the morning.

That night I'm woken up by soft tapping on the door. I flick on a lamp as Gabriel steps into my room.

"Couldn't sleep?" I question him.

"I don't know. I don't even think I tried to sleep yet. Tonight was too good to be true." he looks satisfied.

"Now the world must fall apart," I joke.

"Knowing us it just might." He smiles wickedly then laughs. I can't help but laugh with him. I look over to make sure we haven't woken Anna. She still lays there asleep.

"So what did you want to talk about?" I ask him.

"I thought you had something to say." He knows me so well. My facial features and what they mean.

"Well I was wondering what all happened with the whole fight thing." He looks troubled so I quickly add, "I didn't hear that much about it, and what I did hear didn't sound like you."

I had heard things about the fight. It didn't mean that the information was true, so I wanted to ask Gabriel for the truth. I was sure he wouldn't lie to me about it. The worst thing that he could say was that he started the fight.

Gabriel still looks unsure about it.

"If you don't want to talk about it that's fine too." I say to him.

"I don't really know what all happened. Is it bad to say I don't remember most of it? I was mad. Whoever the other guy was kept acting really stupid. He kept asking me about Shadow. I don't know the guy, and I don't even know who told him about Shadow. I just ended up snapping." He looked down, ashamed.

That had been one of the things that I'd heard from a friend. They said that Gabriel had just been calm and not cared, then something had hit a nerve causing him to lash out at the other boy.

It wasn't like him. It bothered me and I tried to hide it, hoping he wouldn't catch this too. He had enough on his plate.

"You just went off and hit him?" I said surprised.

"Kinda." He admitted sheepishly.

There was more he wasn't telling me. Something that may or may not have anything to do with the fight. Something was bothering him. I didn't want to pry into the situation, but I felt like it would be better if he got whatever it was off his chest. I asked him if he had anything on his mind.

"Well," he started. "I'm scared."

"To tell me?" I asked. He hid his face from me and shook his head no. I got out of bed and walked over to make sure Anna really was asleep. I didn't want her to just be pretending and listening to every word that was said.

"What would scare you?" I asked trying to get some sort of answer out of him.

"I'm scared I'm turning into Dad." He said and then buried his face into his arm.

After so many years of Gabriel and I talking to each other, I had come to the conclusion that he would never be like Dad. He just didn't have it in him. He was a completely different person. There was nothing in him that I had seen that led me to believe he would one day turn into a monster. I also knew he was terrified at the very thought of being remotely like him in any way.

I shook my head no at him when he looked up. A twisted grimace appeared on his face. He grabbed my arm and pulled me through the house until we came to his room. The first thing I noticed was that the one pile of boxes left in the corner was moved out of the way so you could see the wall. Then I noticed the wall itself. What I saw made my jaw drop.

Long scratches covered a large area of the corner. What were they from? It looked like a giant animal had used it as a scratching post. My eyes then fell on a hole in the wall. I saw a knife laying on Gabriel's night stand, then I understood what all the marks really meant.

Knife marks that littered my brother's wall. The hole had probably been made by his fist. The other piles of boxes and objects were probably hiding similar marks. I wondered how he kept this a secret from our mom. Wouldn't she have heard it? Wouldn't she have come in and wondered what the stacks were from?

No, she wouldn't have known. She rarely ever went inside his room anymore. He did his own laundry and kept his room clean. There wasn't any reason for her to examine the inside. He insisted he was mature enough to take care of it himself. All he really was trying to do was hide this.

"Gabriel," I said still shocked, "Why?"

"I told you, I don't know." He started moving the things around to once again conceal the marks and holes. "It just all comes out. I'll be calm and fine. Then I'll have one bad thought and it will get me mad. I can't seem to stop once I start. I blow up. I'll just grab the knife and drill it into the wall. If I don't find the knife right away, I might kick the wall. I don't like to punch it. I wouldn't want Mom to see me with bloody knuckles." His eyes filled with tears.

"Why didn't you say something to me earlier?"

"I'm trying to keep it from people. I don't want anyone hurt by what I do. It wouldn't be worth it. I would never do it to a person. If mom knew, though, she'd never forgive me." I watched as my brother broke down. I never knew he could break. "Hope, I'm scared."

I wanted to hold him. To stop the tears and tell him he wasn't a monster. I wasn't able to form the words though. He wouldn't have believed me anyways.

My poor brother. Pity wasn't going to help him. Was there someone I could tell? Would there be anyone my brother trusted more than me?

"Gabe," my voice was barely audible.

"I don't know what I'm supposed to do. What can I do? I'm horrible, a monster. How can I try to keep everything together when I'm falling apart?"

"Nobody expects you to hold everything around here together. I wouldn't care who you were. No one can do everything. You need a break. Please stop trying so hard." I begged.

"That's all I want to do. I want to keep everyone safe and happy, but all I do is make a mess of things."

"No one expects you to be perfect. We love you Gabriel. I know I do. You're the best brother anyone could ever have asked for. I don't know where we would be without you. You've kept me together for years now. Look at Anna, do you think she would be like this if it wasn't for you?"

He looks at me in disbelief. Somewhere he has to realize I'm not making this up or exaggerating. He has done a lot more for us than anyone else ever has.

"Thanks Hope." He said with a weak smile. After brushing away the tears he hugs me. "Get some sleep. It's not fair for you get be sleep deprived just cause I'm moody."

"I don't mind. I'm always going to be here for you. No matter what happens, you can count on that."

"Alright, alright. Stop worrying so much. That's my job." He pushes me in the direction of my room. "Off to bed."

"I'm going," I yawn. "You get some sleep yourself."

Chapter 6

She looked confused. How can't she be afraid? Look at what I did, I'm a monster. How can't she see the fact that I'm a monster? Is she blind?

How could I have put this on Hope? How could I have showed this to my little sister? I'm supposed to protect her not show her reason to doubt me. How is that helping anyone?

She'll think I need help. I don't want help. I don't need help. Yes, I lost my temper, but I am getting better with it. I know I am.

I don't want to be a monster. I don't want my wife and children to be afraid of me. I didn't want anyone to fear me like that. Especially not my family. Not my two little sisters. Certainly not my mother. Hope would need to promise never to speak a word of this to anyone. She would not be allowed to talk about it, not even with me. I never wanted to hear about it again.

She was disappointed in me. She had to be. There had to be something that she wasn't showing me. Maybe she was worried that it would make me mad and I'd hurt her. I wouldn't blame her if she thought that. I wouldn't blame her at all. She hadn't look like she was mad at me. She hadn't even look disappointed. She looked confused still. That was the only reaction that this caused her.

I was mad though. She was holding her real reactions back from me. She didn't care that I'd picked her to tell because I trusted her more than anyone else. She wouldn't run and tell someone. She wanted me to go and tell someone.

There would only be one way to have her keep it a secret. I would have to stop. Quit cold turkey. I wouldn't let myself lose control like that ever again. If I could promise her that, and mean it, she would keep quiet. Plus, it would give me reason to quit for good. I needed the motive.

I hoped that we hadn't woken someone. I checked in my mother's room, and they were both sound asleep. Then, I waited a half hour before checking on Hope and Anna. They were curled together in the same bed out cold.

How could Hope ask me to go to someone? She knew I wouldn't. That I hated the idea of it. Did she really want me to go somewhere so I could sit down and be told I had a problem? Isn't that a lovely idea for anyone? What was that first step supposed to be? Admit you have an issue. Well I do. I'm not in denial, but I refuse to let anyone handle it for me.

I don't like the way I am. I know I need to change. I will change. For my family, I will change. I will be there for them. Does everyone go through moments like these? It's a wake up call, and a rude one at that, but surely one I won't forget.

These are the times that I know how much Hope helps me. How much worse I would be without her. I know how much she cares about me, but sometimes I need her to show me that I'm not alone.

Hope isn't just my sister. She's my best friend. We've both suffered through the same things. We came out different people because of it. Good people none the less. We'll always be better than Dad. Better morals, better reasoning, better judgement, and a much better temper. We are our own people. Not one person is bound to turn out bad by their blood. I am an individual.

If there is anything that Hope gave me, it's well, hope. She gave me a reason to say I'm not trapped. That I can let this all go. It'll always be part of me, but that doesn't mean I need to be consumed by it. It won't consume me. No matter what, I'll stay on top, and if I go down, I'll fight my way back up. It's possible.

There have been too many times that I've let anger get the best of me. That I let hatred cloud my eyes. Sometimes I just need to let go. It's hard. No one said it would be easy. But if I could fight my way through all of the emotions and let them go, then I will. It'll take a lot of effort, and a lot of drive. Looking around at my family, though, I know they will help me through it. I won't be left alone.

To Hope and me promises cannot be broken once they are made. If I tell her tomorrow that I will try not to loose my temper that way again, you had better believe that I won't break that promise. If all it costs her is to give me the time to prove it to her, then she will be patient with me.

I laid face down on my bed and groaned into my pillow. I hoped that Hope was in her room and not waiting outside listening to what I was doing. I got up and checked. She was still fast asleep in her room. She was probably tired and was thankful to go back to sleep. I'm feeling a bit bad for keeping her awake when she was already so tired.

I returned to my spot on the bed. Thoughts about ending the violent rages filled my head. Never had they happened before recently. It would be a good day, and then I would get home and be alone. For some reason this brought lots of negative thoughts. Then, I just let them all out. But I knew, that since I wasn't always this way, I could go back. I could be me again. How hard could it be? It had to be more difficult to keep going through this. Being someone I definitely wasn't.

I tried to relax, all of my muscles were tense. I need a way to calm myself. Not the way I have been using. That wouldn't work anymore. I couldn't do it while people were home anyway. They would hear for sure. I didn't want anyone else to find out yet. Not til I was ready to tell them. Plus, I'd already given up on that method. It wasn't helping, it was only pushing me farther away from myself.

There was someone else I wanted to tell. Rachel, she was a friend of Hope's. No, friend was an understatement. She was Hope's best friend. They should've been sisters. She seemed to be a great listener. If there was something Hope needed to get off her chest and she didn't want to tell me, Rachel probably knew what it was. Maybe if I told her, she would know what to say.

Could I trust her enough? Would she take it better than Hope did?

There was a reason I was glad Rachel wasn't related to us. I liked her. A lot. Probably a lot more than I should. I am kinda worried. What if I only trust her because I have feelings for her? She didn't seem like one to betray me, but I've been wrong before.

An hour passed and my head was still swimming with thoughts. I needed to go to bed. I rolled over and searched blindly under my bed with my hand. I found what I was looking for. I pulled the bottle out from beneath the bed. It was a water bottle filled with a heavy liquor I'd found in the basement. I'd only taken a little to begin with. When no one noticed it was gone I started taking larger amounts at a time.

Hope would kill me if she knew. Without a doubt in my mind, she would strangle me. Hope would chew me out for weeks. I wouldn't be surprised if she never talked to me again. It wasn't like I didn't deserve it anyway. I wondered if she would even care after today.

I opened the bottle and took a large mouthful. After I swallowed I waited and started to feel a warm feeling spread through my body. It felt good at first. Then I started to feel sick. Not from the liquor, but from my conscience. I couldn't actually believe I was drinking. For the same reasons my father had no doubt.

This was the only promise that I ever made to Hope and broke. It was the worst one I probably ever could break. It wasn't like I drank often. Only as a last resort. At the very most, maybe once a month. Once in a lifetime was one time too many though.

I closed the bottle tight. "I don't need you." I said to the dark liquid. "I never did. I never will again."

Hot fresh tears spilled out. I threw the bottle in disgust. I would throw it out tomorrow. I would never bring myself to this low of a point again. Why was I being so stupid lately? Stupidity wasn't what worried me. I was so scared that I was getting more and more like Dad. I wanted to get rid of the thought. I wasn't him. Hope said that I never would be.

Another thing I would quit cold. Should I start making a list? No, that wouldn't help me.

"Never again will I be in this place. I'm waking up." I said to myself.

I still couldn't sleep. Instead of finding peace I was kept up by one thought. Something I hadn't done in a while. It had been far too long.

Climbing out of bed, I went over to my closet. I pushed aside shoes and large cardboard boxes until I found the object I was looking for. I pulled the black rectangle out of it's home in the back corner of my closet. It was about the size of a shoe box, only slightly shorter and flatter.

I opened my box. It contained everything that I held near and dear to me. Anything that was sentimental to me went in here. I never wanted to forget anything. I had a baseball that my dad and I used to play with, and pictures of relatives and friends with huge smiles plastered to our faces. The smiles weren't fake, or forced into place, they were natural and reached all the way into our eyes.

Finally, I found what I was looking for. I pulled out the small leather draw string pouch. Bringing the pouch up to my face, I inhaled deeply through my nose. It smelled like pipe tobacco and spices that you would find in the kitchen. It had been my pap's cross. He had given it to me after my parents divorce, and told me that if I was ever having a hard time, all I had to do was ask God to fix it.

I pulled the tiny steel cross out. It had been made by my uncle. I pressed the cool metal to my lips. I felt like a little kid again. It made me smile. All the thoughts that filled my head were full of smiles and laughter. Easier issues with easier ways to overcome my trouble's. Right now, I needed a little help though. There was only one person who could help me with something like this.

Tonight I did something that I haven't even thought about doing for a couple years now. I closed my eyes folded my hands around the cross and prayed. I asked God for help. I asked him to forgive me for how I have been acting. For him to keep me strong so I wouldn't fall apart on my family.

If I was ever tempted to drink again, I would think back on this. I would think back on how it would affect my family if they found out. It wasn't too late for me to make myself a better person. I didn't have to hurt them the way Dad had. I wouldn't have to torture my future with being an alcoholic. I'm my own person. I am better than that.

Chapter 7

The bottle runs dry. I laugh, it's the laugh you expect to hear in an institute. I stop for a second when the thought crosses my mind. Then I laugh again. It's so funny to me for no reason at all. I look around and see all the bottles and cans that lay around me. Oh my dear friends. One is just never enough is it?

I talk to myself out loud, "I could sure use a cleaning lady." Again I'm thrown into a fit of hysterics. I collapse back on the couch. After the laughter finishes my whole body is rocked by spasms. I cough and grab a towel off the floor to cover my mouth. When I pull it away, I find that it's stained with red. I should quit smoking. I wanted to try before, but gave up before I even started. So much for sticking with it.

Wasn't much worth in quitting something you were good at right? Well, this is what I was good at. I throw the bloody towel into the corner on top of a pile of clothes that should've been washed weeks ago. Never got around to it I guess.

I'd never get someone to help me clean this mess. I'd never even try to clean it myself. It has been like this for years. It gets worse everyday. It has turned into a dungeon for me to rot away in. I don't even have enough sense to care about it. Another smile twists it's way onto my face.

I turn on the music to a cheery song and start to sing along. I get up and stumble around. I almost fall into the pile of clothes.

"Well, well, well, that wouldn't smell like a spring time meadow would it?" I jump up and down and spin around laughing till it hurts. After a while I go sit back down on the couch. I look around. Home. If you could consider this place home. There was no home. Not for anyone. Especially not for me.

I get up and move a couple steps before I stumble and fall to the ground. I feel a massive headache coming on. When it hits, I lay on the ground. It feels like my head is going to split in two. My mind throws me in and out of reality. I can't remember where I am anymore. There are no thoughts for me to hold onto. Everything just passes by in a blur. There is nothing I can begin to understand.

I think I'm spinning around in circles. It feels like it, but when I open my eyes everything seems like it's still. Maybe the whole room is spinning. I'm tired so I close my eyes. May as well sleep here.

I think I'm dreaming. Shapes and places pass before my eyes. I am either dreaming or dying. Does it matter which? I try to fall asleep on the floor. Each time my eyes shut, I am greeted by a memory. I don't want to remember. I want to go back to sleep. Sleep is better than this. Anything is better than this.

I open my eyes back up, but around me things are getting blurry. Around the edges of my vision things go dark, then black. The blackness works it's way from the edges to the center. Right before I pass out, I see a memory of a woman.

She is so beautiful. I know her and she knows me too. We haven't talked for so long. I try to go over to her. I miss her. I want to see and talk to her again. I don't remember where I have seen her before.

"Who are you?" I ask. Maybe she is a ghost. She looks more like an angel. Maybe an angel of death come to take me away.

She watches me for a moment. I still can not place her. I want to go touch her. Make sure that she's real. She isn't though. This woman would never come to see me. Why am I crying? I watch this angel as she turns to leave me alone in my suffering and filth. She wants to leave me here, she wants me to stay and suffer alone.

"Wait, please don't go." I want her to stay. Maybe if I can convince her, she'll stay to comfort me.

When she looks back, there is no regret in her eyes. She shakes her head slowly. Her decision is no. She will not stay here, nor will she try to help me. She hasn't come to take me away from this. She won't help me escape.

"Please, please I'm begging you. Don't go." She already is gone though. I'm left alone once again.

I cry until there is nothing left to cry about. Once I feel empty, I know I am alone. No one wants to be here for me. Even Heather has left. She no longer wants me. Again I ruin lives. It's like I can't stop. Now I have five children out there. Will I ever even see the fifth? Does it matter anymore?

It would probably be better if I didn't. If the baby was raised far away and never had to meet me. I don't even want the child to know who I am. Every baby deserves a happy family. I am able to cry again now. I laugh at myself too. That is something I will never be able to provide.

Somehow I manage to get up. My stomach lurches. I puke all over the floor. I wipe my face on my shirt. I manage to go back to the couch. I fall down onto it. Next to me is a spilled bottle. I am laying in the mess. I don't care. I drink what is left from another bottle on the floor.

In my mind, I beg God to just to end it. Kill me now I beg. Take me away. I don't want this anymore. I don't want life. I find another half empty bottle and swallow all that is left in it. Then I finally find relief in passing out.

Chapter 8

I feel really lost in school. Even Rachel gives me space to think by myself for a while. I am confused, annoyed and fearful. Gabriel is still kicked out of school. He'll be back Tuesday. I feel guilty, but I am relieved that he isn't around me right now. I need time to think. I can think at home, but I want some time to do so alone.

Distracted, I stop working and look around the room. I should try to get my homework done now. There are just too many thoughts in my head though. I take a breath and clear my head. I work hard and think about nothing but the sheet of paper in front of me. The bell rings just as I finish.

I rush downstairs to study hall. This will be my time to sort out my thoughts. I choose the library today. Fortunately it is all but empty. No one will bother me. I take out a piece of paper and a pen. I start to make a list of things that have happened lately. I write down that Gabriel and I talked. Under that I write down different thoughts that bother me.

Gabriel is afraid of being like our dad. That's how he is affected by everything that has happened due to our dad. The late bell rings and my pen is still scribbling down every thought I have. If Gabriel is affected, then am I affected? If so, how? I worry about how much I was affected, and how much has stuck with me. Even more pressing, what has stayed with me and become something worse?

It's not that I am constantly bothered about things that have to do with our dad. The weeks that go by and we don't see him make everything a lot easier. The months that go by without so much as a call turn out to be pure joy instead of frustration. I make note of these thoughts on my list and move on.

Without thinking to, I write down that it would be a good idea to take away Gabriel's knife. I go to scratch it out but stop. It isn't really that bad of an idea. I could ask him about it later. Say that if it was out of sight, he wouldn't dwell on it as much. It would be a heathy decision not to keep his knives around him.

I really hoped he has cooled down enough that he wouldn't take it as me saying I didn't trust him. I do trust him. That was the only reason I hadn't told our mom. I knew Gabriel would change. It wouldn't be a problem any longer.

As I go over my list, Rachel takes a chair across from me. She doesn't talk at first; which is why I don't notice her until I look up from my paper.

"So are you feeling any better about Shadow?" She says it like she's trying to break the ice for something more serious. She isn't trying to hide the fact that something else is on her mind. And if she's not trying to hide it, that means she'll be talking about it soon.

"Yeah, I am starting to say that it actually happened. I haven't been looking for him around the house anymore. I don't expect him to be there when I get home from school anymore. My mom's boyfriend actually got a gravestone made for him.

You should've seen my mom when she got it." I said.

"That was nice of him. At least he's trying to help with the situation." Rachel answered. She knew how hard he was trying for everyone but didn't mention it. "What is wrong with Gabriel lately?" She finally said.

Rachel didn't beat around the bush. If there was something she wanted to know she got right to the point pretty fast. She didn't jump down your throat or anything. I was glad about that. I respected her a lot for it too. Rachel was really good with people. I couldn't wait to see where her life took her. I always knew it would be somewhere good. She would do well.

"Did you notice something?" I wanted to know what she had seen first.

"I don't know if I should tell you if he hasn't." She whispered. She wouldn't want to break a person's trust unless she thought it was very important to tell someone. "You know that he's been talking to me lately, right?"

This is one of the thousands of reasons that I trust my best friend; she is always honest. If there was something she couldn't tell you about, she wouldn't lie and say that she didn't know, she would just tell you that she wasn't allowed to say. That was her nice way of putting things. She could also inform a person on how they had absolutely no right to know. Rachel was never mean about it. She was only ever honest. Very blunt.

"Don't worry, I kinda figured that you did. He likes you, and you're a sucker for a cute guy." I smiled at her. I didn't want her to feel stressed that she told me. I thought maybe she'd feel better if she knew we were still able to joke around.

"No way, I do not like him!" She tried to defend herself, but the attempt fell flat. She looked both ways and then back at me. "Okay, maybe a little. Does he really like me?"

"Gabriel has no girlfriend and has followed you around like a lost puppy every time you've come over for the past two years." I teased her.

"He's been different lately." She said, and her face fell with her eyes. "He's been so angry lately, I just can't figure out why. I finally worked up the nerve to ask if something was wrong let alone what it actually was that bothered him." She looked like she could've cried. She hated when people were in pain.

Rachel pulled her phone out of her purse and scrolled through the messages, when she found the one she wanted, she passed me her phone under the table. I looked at who sent it, and I wasn't surprised to find that it was Gabriel. Then I looked at the message. I read it again.

I can't take it anymore. I want him to leave us alone. I want him to go away.

I passed the phone back to her. She selected another message and showed it to me. This one bothered me. This one was a picture. It was of the same wall Gabriel had showed me. The same cuts were etched in the wall. The same hole showed were his foot had gone through. The words at the bottom of the screen jumped out at me.

Don't let me be like him.

"I promised him he's not. He's never been anything like your dad. The marks don't prove anything." Rachel said defensively. She was trying to protect him. She didn't need to defend him from me. Gabriel needed defended from himself. I wasn't going to stab my brother in the back.

I was surprised Gabriel had made a point to show Rachel. It was one thing to tell her about how he was feeling and what he had done as a result. It was completely different to show her something like this. I didn't want Rachel to make it her problem. It wouldn't be right to think that it was. She just helped me so much that maybe she thought Gabriel needed help with it too. After all, it was the same situation that we were going through.

"The knife marks scared me. Do you know about them?" She whispered quietly across to me, she was concerned.

"Yes, he just showed them to me last night." I still couldn't believe he had gone and showed her after getting mad at me for trying to be there for him. "I've been worried about it all day."

"At least he's being open about it. It could be a lot worse. Especially if he was still trying to hide it." She said. I was in agreement with her there. There was no need for him to have to hide this. She frowned and looked down.

"Rachel?" I asked, "Do me a favor would you?"

"Sure, what is it?"

"Keep an eye on Gabe for a while. Let me know if he's venting, okay?"

"Sure, but Hope? You watch out for him too, okay?" She asked. As if I wasn't doing that round the clock now anyways.

I nodded though. I would be looking out for my brother. I was worried about him. The bell rang and we left. We would probably talk about this again soon. I really didn't want it to be too soon. I was ready to put this all behind me. There would be some things that needed to be taken care of first. Then we could all look back and say we made it through another hard time.

○●○

I went to get Anna again for Gabriel. Figured I may as well try and help him relax. He didn't need to stress or worry anymore than need be. It was bad enough that he had so much pressure on him that he snapped and got suspended. He didn't need to stress while he was home too.

I walked in and smelled whatever my mom was cooking. It made my mouth water. I recognized what it was. Vegetable soup. She had gotten the recipe off of her dad. Pap made the best food ever. No one could compare.

I loved my grandparents. I wanted to visit them soon. They didn't live far away. I could be there everyday and still feel like I wasn't there enough.

"How was your day?" She asked when I walked into the kitchen.

"Nothing I could complain about for more than ten minutes, so pretty good. How about yours?" I laughed a little and it felt good to shrug off some of the day's worries. I would have to deal with it later, but a few minutes of down time would be nice.

"Pretty boring, and then it got pretty stupid. I'm really getting to be sick of how people handle their business."

We started to joke around and I helped her make dinner. It was nice to joke about the little things in life. We never really did anymore for some reason. It felt good to just sit back, and relax, and act like life was normal. Whatever could be considered normal anymore. Did anyone have a "normal" life?

Anna chose that moment to intrude. She told us all about her day. We also got a very detailed account of how a new boy in her class had offered her a cookie at lunch. Young love, so beautiful. Anna was such a little flirt. She tried to be too. She knew she was adorable and fully used that to her advantage.

Anna was an angel look alike with her straight blonde hair and dimples. The only thing missing to complete the look was a set of downy white feathered wings. That would top it off. She would be absolutely irresistible.

"Boys are nasty," She finished her story with.

Oh my sweet little sister. I couldn't wait for the day she found one of those "nasty boys" to be her boyfriend. I would have to remind her of what she just told us. I couldn't wait to find her kissing one of those "nasty" little boys and sit him down with Gabriel for a nice little chat. I rolled my eyes and my mom laughed. I left the kitchen to go find something to do.

When I walked into the living room I noticed mom's boyfriend was home. He had a long busy week, and was grumpy because he would have another long week. He didn't sit around in an office all day. He did work hard. I was glad for that at least. He put a great deal of effort into his work.

I found Gabriel out back. He was hard at work trimming bushes. Sweat covered his face. I wondered why Mom had made him do this so late in the year. Probably just something else to make him work while he was home.

"I see mom is still putting you to work." I told him.

"Yeah," He looked at me right before snapping off a large part of the bush. "Apparently the punk I hit had to go to the hospital. Having to and wanting to are subjective terms though. I think he just wanted me in even more trouble if something got broken."

"Did you break anything?" I asked. I doubted Gabriel would break someone else's bones, but he had been doing a lot of things that I found out of character lately.

"No, but it still wasn't a pleasant experience for him."

I wanted to laugh, but I didn't know how Gabriel would take it right now. I didn't know if he was still mad at me or not. I hoped not. Me trying to help him wasn't going to be easy if he was going to try to keep his guard up.

Gabriel set down the trimmers and turned to look at me. He wiped the sweat off his face with his shirt.

"Hope, I'm glad that I told you everything. I'm sorry I got so mad at you. I was expecting you to judge me. When you didn't, I didn't know what to think. I really screwed up." He said. So he wasn't mad anymore. That was good. I'm glad it wouldn't be a battle that we would have to come back to later. Gabriel was taking responsibility for what he had said and done.

"I talked to Rachel about everything too." He said. He watched me, trying to gage my reaction. He wanted to know how much she had told me. "I know you'll say I only told her because I like her, but that's not it. You trust her. I figured if you can tell her everything she might be willing to listen to me too. You trust her opinion. You believe in what she says. You take her advice. She actually had some that I could use. It helped me, talking to her that is.

You were right. I did need to talk to someone about everything."

"Honestly, as bad as letting that happened is, you are still taking it out on yourself too hard. You're always too hard on yourself in my opinion. You've been so worried about every thing with Dad. Your letting it all come down on you at once." I said. I wanted to help Gabriel too. I wanted him to be happy.

"Like I said, maybe your right. Maybe all I really need to do is just talk to someone. I talked to Rachel and it helped. It felt so good to just let it out. I thought about maybe talking to mom." He said. I knew he wouldn't want to, but he knew it was a good idea. She was going through all of this with us. We couldn't exclude her from the situation, likewise she can't exclude us. She never has before, so what would make her start now?

"Good, see Gabe? Everything will be alright." I smiled.

"Me and mom fought again today though." This is why he wasn't happy.

"What happened?"

"I was all stressed out thinking about what would happen if I talked to her. What if she thinks I'll turn out like him Hope? What if she doesn't want me here because of it?" He told me. Poor Gabriel. Once you took one thing off his plate a dozen more problems seemed to appear. "You weren't home when she threatened to kick me out of the house if I couldn't get my act together."

I looked at Gabriel confused. Our mom wouldn't really say that would she? Could she even say such a thing to Gabriel? Could she say something like that to any of us?

"When did she say that to you?" My voice was defensive. I wanted to defend Gabriel from Mom, and Mom from Gabriel. I couldn't defend both of them at the same time though.

"When you and Anna were at school. She was mad about me still being suspended. Her and her boyfriend had been fighting earlier." He said solemnly.

"At least Dad didn't call about this weekend." I said trying to cheer him up.

"That's right," He said with a smile. "I forgot it was Friday." Gabriel checked his phone and smiled. "No missed calls on my phone."

"So why are you the only one who calls Dad, and he only calls you?" I asked, trying to keep a conversation going.

"I never really thought about it. I guess when we were little I was the only one with a phone, so I was the only one he could call. It must have just stuck even after you got yours. Why, do you want the job?" He laughed and I couldn't tell if he meant it or not. The look in his eyes said he'd give up the responsibility in a heart beat. I'm sure he would too.

Soon we were called in for dinner. It had been a long day, and I was tired, so I decided to head to bed early. I crawled between the sheets and sat there for a minute. Things were looking up in retrospect. That was enough to keep me going. I laid down then. My head hit the pillow and I was out almost instantly.

Rough breathing fills my ears. My heart is pounding so hard in my chest. I am trying to escape. Heavy boots sink into the earth right behind me. They are too close. Pushing hard I fly forward in a last ditch effort. I can feel it before it even happens. I'm mid stride in the air when I'm hit in the side and fall hard against the damp ground. A huge figure lurches at me and traps me before I'm able to get up. My neck burns with a searing pain as strong hands twist me and bend me in unnatural ways. I try to scream and struggle free, but I can't. The pain is too much.

I feel how tight the hands are around my throat as they turn me into a pretzel. Another set of screams fill my lungs. I go to let them out, maybe someone will hear them this time. Maybe someone will finally come and help me.

Right as I go to scream a boot goes into me. I feel all the air rush out of my lungs. Please have mercy. Please God if this is my end make it swift. Please do not let me suffer. I don't want my life to end this way.

118

I bring faces into my thoughts and say goodbye as the next one snaps into focus.

I jolt upright and fight off the feelings of the dream. I take deep breaths letting my body know that I am able to breathe. I'm on the floor in a ball. My shoulders are tight. I tilt my head side to side and rejoice when I don't feel pain. Only the soreness and stiffness from being in the uncomfortable position. It was a dream. Only another sickeningly real dream.

There are few dreams I remember when I wake up. Usually the ones I am able to bring back are the ones that stir emotion. This dream brought up an emotion, fear. I had been trapped in a nightmare.

The screams hadn't been mine. Something in my head told me that they belonged to another. I knew who's they were. They were my mother's screams.

I manage to fall back asleep. The dreams are done haunting me for the night. I stay under for the rest of the night. I felt relieved when I woke up and remembered it was Saturday. The weekends always brought joy. A chance to recharge and prepare for another round. It was nice though.

After fifteen minutes I settled on a pair of running shorts and a compression tee. I found my mom in the kitchen and told her I was going for a walk. I pulled on my shoes and headed out the door. I jogged for the first half hour then took a break.

It felt nice to burn off some energy. Running was always a reliable way to do that. I hadn't left to blow off energy. Actually, I had come out to think. I needed to find a way to get rid of my nightmares.

I started walking to Rachel's and called her when I was close. She met me in front of her house and we walked together. I told her about my dream. I told her about maybe trying to find closure by talking to my dad.

"If you already have a plan for closure why don't you try it? Something is better than nothing isn't it?" She asked.

I wondered if she realized it wasn't that easy. It wasn't exactly something we chatted about. Dad never spoke about it. It was like it never happened. Did he ever think about it? Did he ever regret what he had done to his family?

"What do I say to him?" Where to begin would be a better question I thought to myself. If Rachel couldn't help me figure this out, no one could. She knew the most about the situation. She looked at me for a second, then dropped her eyes. She was thinking hard trying to figure out the best way to go about doing this.

"Hope, you know I care about you. There really isn't anything I can tell you to do other than be honest with him about what you're thinking. Don't hold anything back, or you'll never get it out. It might be a one shot deal." She stopped when I looked puzzled. "Do you think he'll ever want to talk about it again? You may only get one chance to catch him off guard and get him to admit things."

"You're probably right there," I said. Rachel had a point. It was most likely going to be an all or nothing kind of thing. I wouldn't be able to let him stay quiet

121

through this speech. This time I needed to be heard.

When we finally made the loop back to her house, I pulled her in for a big hug.

"Thank you for everything Rachel. I'm gonna talk to Gabriel about all of this and see what he says. If I do this, it can't just be me. He has to do it with me."

"Definitely include him," she said with a smile, then she gave me a push. "Don't thank me yet. You can thank me once I've been proven right."

Chapter 9

I slowly open my eyes. It doesn't feel like morning. It doesn't really feel like anytime at all. It feels like I've been sucked into a black hole, chewed up, and spit out. I get to my feet and check the time. It's already six in the afternoon.

I need to clean these bottles out of here eventually. I grab an arm full and go to throw them out. When I make it to the garbage can, I see the paper is still on the ground. Flipping it open to the front page, I jump a little. It isn't the story about the fire killing a family of five, or the recent string of violent robberies that gives me chills. It's the date. Something small and insignificant.

A Saturday morning shouldn't scare anyone. Unless the last day you remember is Thursday. It can't already be Saturday. Could I really have been out for over thirty-six hours? I throw the paper away and head back inside.

As I walk into the kitchen, it feels like the room is spinning. I pass the headache off as not eating for too long. The room starts tilting. Bracing myself against the table, I close my eyes and pinch the bridge of my nose. When I open my eyes, I'm face first on the ground.

I have a hard time believing I'm in my house. This doesn't feel like a home. It feels like I'm trapped. The walls are closing in on me. I can't move. I just watch as they get closer to me, threatening to crush me.

Warm blood flows from a gash from my head. I must have hit it off the counter on my way down. For a while I try to be still there. It seems all I can do is sit there and tremble. I feel like I'm going to be sick. I still can't get up, and end up emptying the contents of my stomach on the floor and myself.

It burns coming up just as it did going down. Soon I manage to get to my feet. Then a searing pain hits. It starts in my heart and works it's way into my head. I've never even imagined pain like this. It feels like someone lit fireworks off in my head. Right where my heart should be, it feels like someone started a fire. It keeps building; engulfing my heart in an inferno.

I barely make it to the phone and dial 911. The operator wants to know what my emergency is.

"Please help me," I plead half in hysterics. I force out my address before everything around me starts to get dark. I'm not able to make out the words on the other end of the line. In my head I'm begging God for mercy. Something tells me it's too little too late. Maybe I never had a chance to begin with.

Chapter 10

I feel better. I finally feel like myself for the first time in a long time. This might not seem like a huge deal. It might not seem like such an overwhelming accomplishment. Overall, I just feel like I can be happy with myself.

I haven't touched my knife. In fact, I gave it to Hope so I wouldn't be tempted. She told me she would hide it just in case. I was glad she had done it for me. Not just because it helped, but because it showed she really did care what happened to me. If my sister could have so much faith in me, then I was going to show Hope that I could be a better person.

I had said something like that to Hope. She had told me that she didn't want me to show her that I could be a better person. She wanted me to show myself that I was a better person. Personally, I think showing both of us is a good idea.

I haven't felt overly stressed lately, and I haven't been so hard on myself for everything. The best part is that I haven't felt like I need to stay calm. There have been no breakdowns lately. I couldn't ask for anything more.

Venting actually helped. Hope helped me. I wish there was a way that I could show her how much it had meant to me. Rachel had helped tremendously, too. Maybe Hope wasn't the only one who had put their faith in me. Maybe my family weren't the only ones that I needed to show I was a better person.

I find the last of the baseball cards that Dad and I used to collect together. I put them in a box with the rest of the things that make me think about him. I'm going to get over this, and then I'm going to get through this. Since I have the chance, I may as well take it.

Hope and I had a pretty important talk when she got home from her walk this morning. We finally made the decision. We were finally going to get closure with our dad, and we were going to do it the only way we could think of.

We were going to confront our dad. We were still trying to convince our mom it was a good idea. We were going to sit him down and get everything out. Finally, that night would have some light shown on it, and we wouldn't let him slink his way out of talking this time. All of the thoughts about how he had changed our lives would finally come out. Every nightmare about the people we might turn out to be would be forgotten.

Mom wasn't sold at first, but we convinced her that it was something that needed to be done. We deserved answers. We needed them, or at least to say, we had made one last attempt.

Hope had been right all along. I didn't need the revenge I had been looking for, and craving, for so long. I didn't need his love or his acceptance. It felt good to finally see a way to get everything over with. Maybe it was just because we were all so excited, but I felt like this would finally be the end.

He would get two choices: one, explain to us everything that had happened that night and try to fix things, or two, prove to us that he was the worthless piece of scum we already saw him as. Either way, things would be settled. It was about time things started going right.

Chapter 11

Lights are flashing all around me. It feels like something is trying to split my skull in two. People are working over me, and I can't tell what is going on. All of their words jumble together, and I can't make sense of what they are asking me. I try to look around. Silver tools are laying around me.

The picture clears up some. I know where I am to some extent. I'm in an ambulance on my way to the hospital. I still don't know what's wrong. All I know is everything hurts.

Instead, I try to picture an hour glass and fill it with the time I have left. It keeps switching between being much too full, and having the last grain of sand free falling downwards.

The voices start to get louder, and we come to a stop. The doors fly open, and I'm rushed inside. People press against walls and try to give us enough room to get by. I catch the eye of a nurse, she shakes her head as we go past with her mouth hanging open in shock. Her eyes are wide as she takes in the sight of me. It was such a small gesture. But I remembered it. She was the angel from my dream. She was the one who had no hope for me. The one who turned away and wouldn't come back to save me.

It was also the angel whom I had tried to break. The poor innocent angel that I wanted to see fall from the sky, never to fly again. I remembered all too clearly her screams of pain. Now she would get to listen to mine. Oh, my sweet little angel. I would've given up on me, too, long before you had.

Chapter 12

Gabriel and I are finally on the same page. Today, we talked to our mom before she left for the hospital for work. Gabriel and I had told her that we were going to talk to Dad about the night he had tried to kill her. After a while, she agreed that we could try. She also stressed that we shouldn't be disappointed if things didn't end the way we wanted them to.

I have thought of so many questions to ask him. I wondered if he would answer all of them. I wondered if he would answer any at all. He had to have something to say. The main thing I want to ask him is something I already know the answer to. Something that I want him to prove me wrong about. I want to ask him if he really had it in him to kill our mom. What would have given him reason to do such a thing in the first place?

There is another question that pushes it's way to the center of my thoughts, begging me for attention. It scares me and I push it away, but after a few minutes, it always comes back. It's the question that has plagued me with nightmares for half of my life. If my dad had it in himself to kill our mother, his wife, then what would he have done with his three small children? We may not have seen anything, but we had heard it. Would we have been condemned to death as well?

What would have stopped him? Would he have gotten rid of any evidence? Then what would have happened? Would he have gone off to jail? Somehow I think he would've gotten away with it anyhow. He would've escaped fate just like he always seemed to.

Anna looks so unaffected by all of this. Gabriel and I briefed her on our plan after she woke up. I didn't think she had many questions for him. I figured I should ask her about it though.

"Anna, if you could ask Dad any question, and he had to answer you honestly, what would you ask him?"

Anna sat still for a few seconds. Her face turned red slowly and tears filled her eyes. I walked over and sat next to her so I could brush her tears away.

"I would ask him why he didn't want to be here with us." The tears came faster now. They fell in a steady stream down her face. "Doesn't he love us enough to stay?"

I almost cried myself. She didn't need to see me cry. She didn't need to worry anymore than she already had. I felt bad for putting more on her tiny shoulders. I wiped all the tears from her eyes and settled her down. She got quiet and started playing with her toys again.

I took the oppurtunity to leave the room. Anna hadn't said anything wrong. It had been one of the questions that I had in my head during the past few hours. I never would have dreamed that my poor little sister would have the same thoughts haunting her as well. The answer she wanted to know came from a question I thought I could never, let alone should ever, ask about.

A lot had happened these past few days. Our lives had already been changed, but it felt like they were about to again. In the past few days, Gabriel had given up, and then found the strength he needed to continue.

Gabriel was feeling much better. He wasn't the same. At the same time he hadn't really changed all that much. He didn't change who he was. It was more like he was regaining control of the person he had been. When had he changed in the first place? Why hadn't I noticed something like that?

It was because he changed when Dad decided to change our lives. The reason I hadn't noticed was because I was too caught up in how I was changing myself. I was growing up too fast and not paying attention to the people around me.

Gabriel became someone who anyone would be lucky to have. He would be strong and supportive. He would make himself the backbone of his family. Just like he was our backbone now.

Anna, my sweet little sister has also changed. As much as I want to deny it, and as much as I want to say our situation won't affect her life, it already has. She never got to have a father. None of us did. But, Gabriel and I still had more of a memory of a dad than she did. Instead she has our pap for guidance and support. She has our grandma to tell stories to and play with.

Even our mother has changed. That isn't really much of a surprise though. Maybe she'll never be able to give her heart to another. Maybe she'll never understand what it feels like to be loved and love back unconditionally. But she loves us, and we love her. She knows what that feels like, and that's all any one of us will ever really need.

Mom will never be able to go back. Her neck is permanently injured. She will always have to carry around that pain. I will always stand by her though. No matter what has happened to her, she never let it put her down. She never sat back and let things happen. She always pushed forward.

I will always stand by my mom. I don't care what happens between us. I don't care what we fight about. We will always be there for one another.

She had to put up with a monster. She went through hell and back, and still managed to raise three children. Three children who turned out very well. She fought through everything. Things that would break most people. And she still managed to come out on top.

Even though I don't want it to be true, I've been affected too. I get upset easily when people show me they can't be trusted. I always want to help my friends because I can't stand to know someone is in pain. I grew up fast. I had to learn that the world isn't the happy place we wish it could be. I know I'm not the first one to realize that. I know people go through worse things. I'm one of the lucky ones. I can see the world through my own eyes without having it break me.

There is another reason I feel I'm lucky. I know I'm my own person. I know I don't have to grow up to be my dad. My nights won't be filled with dreams of regret and sorrow because of what I've turned myself into. I'll always be able to look in the mirror in the morning.

I will not be one of the people who lives their life full of regret and misery. I will not hold things back. I'm going to get everything off my chest. I will not break. But you had better know I will always stand strong.

Chapter 13

Today is the big day. Today we are going to get answers. We are going to call Dad today and tell him to meet us at the park. We'll lay it all out. No going back, whatever we say, we're going to have to make it worth it.

I'm scared and really nervous. My stomach is full of butterflies. Butterflies are pretty; however, there is nothing pretty about what I'm going to do. Worms would be a much better comparison. Yes, my stomach feels like it's full of worms.

I have only vented once like this before. I've yelled, but never had a central point to focus on. The message was never really clear. Basically, all I had ever done was rant.

For some reason everything about today makes me think about a couple years ago. I tried "getting through" to my dad. I vented, but it didn't work. Before, I didn't vent to try to help anyone. I did it out of anger. I wanted him to be in pain. To share the hurt I was going through. I wanted to watch him squirm as he broke and took responsibility for everything he caused.

This time I have reasons. This time I'm not trying to prove a point. This time I'm trying to help myself and my family. I don't think I want to see my dad break anymore. Right now, I just want him to tell us he knows he screwed up and why.

So what happens if he doesn't understand, and denies everything? Then it wasn't ever worth trying in the first place. No matter what happens, I know I'm going to find some kind of closure today. This is what Gabriel, Anna, and I have been waiting for. It's the last time I'll set myself up for disappointment from him.

I watch as Gabriel storms down the stairs. Why is he mad? Today is not a day for senseless anger.

"Of all the lousy times." I hear him muttering as he gets closer.

"What is it?"

"I've called him at least a dozen times." He says. "No answer, and the voice mail is full. Of all the days for him to ignore us."

"Is mom home from work yet?" I asked.

"Yes, she called late after you and Anna were asleep. She had to work a night-shift because so many people can't go to work because they're sick. Sick people working in a hospital kinda defeats the purpose. I think she got home around three or so. She sounded off though. I think she was worried about the day. She should be fine now since we aren't going anywhere."

"Alright, I didn't want her to worry. She is gonna be exhausted today anyways." I say. I don't want her to try to stay awake just because she thinks something might go wrong.

We turn when we hear the phone ringing in the kitchen. Gabriel rushes inside to pick it up so it doesn't wake anyone. I follow him in. By the time I get there, Gabriel is just hanging up. He's staring at the floor and clutching the counter.

"Gabriel," I panic, "what happened? What's wrong?" He looks like he's going to be sick. He stands there too long without answering and I push him. He barely moves.

"Knock it off Hope." He says, but I barely hear him.

"I would if you didn't look like you just watched someone get hit by a car. What happened Gabriel? Who was it?" He has me worried now.

"It was the hospital." He said slowly.

"They don't want mom back do they? Gabriel spit it out already." I'm about ready to start shoving him again.

"No Hope, they didn't call about mom." His eyes focus and he watches me wanting to know my reaction for whatever it is that he's about to say. "They called to tell us that Dad had been admitted. That's why he hasn't answered my calls."

My face probably holds the same mask as Gabriel's, confusion and shock.

I run upstairs yelling for my mother. Gabriel catches my arm half way up the stairs and spins me around.

"What are you doing?" He demands.

"She might know something Gabriel. She works there. Maybe someone noticed him and told her."

"No, she would've told me about it when she called."

"What would she have said? After working so late? You really think she was gonna just say that? She probably had no idea how to say it." I say. I just hope he can see my logic. I know what he's thinking though. Even if it was late, why wouldn't she have told us something?

Mom came down the stairs in a robe. She looked between Gabriel and I. She looked worried.

"Is everything alright?" She looked us up and down. "No one is hurt?"

Gabriel looked at her for a long moment.

"Nobody here is hurt," he said, "but the hospital just called to let us know that Dad has been admitted. It's bad. I guess he suffered a heart attack."

My jaw dropped. Gabriel hadn't mentioned that he knew what had happened. It felt like a stone had been dropped in my stomach. It wasn't because I was worried. I felt sick because it felt like I already had known this would happen. I had been right about the feeling that things were going to be finished. I never would've imagined things to go like this. The stone doubled in size.

"Did you know?" I asked my mother.

"Last night they rushed in a man. He looked at me when he passed. I thought I was just overly tired when I thought I had seen him. I must not have been. It must have actually happened." She trailed off. It looked like she had seen a ghost.

Anna hobbled down the stairs with a blanket in her arms. She found us in the kitchen. She rubbed the last of the sleep from her eyes.

"Is breakfast ready?" She asked in a tired voice. Looking up, the mood of the room finally seemed to settle on her. She frowned. "Is everybody okay?"

"Take us to the hospital." Gabriel said pulling on his jacket and shoes. He could have driven himself, but looking at him, I doubt if he could've if he had wanted to.

Mom explained to Anna what was going on as she drove. If Dad was going to die, there were some things that needed to be said. Maybe we couldn't have the big vent that we wanted. But we couldn't keep this all in. If he died, then he would die knowing everything he put us through.

My whole body was trembling by the time we pulled into the hospital. Fight or flight. I couldn't run away from this. Instead, I was running right into it.

We found his room quickly. Even though I was somewhat prepared to talk to him, I was not ready for what I walked into. There were tubes everywhere. I wasn't new to the hospital set up. I was new to the helpless way the man in the bed looked. It didn't make me smile to see him this way. Gabriel looked cold, but he didn't seem to particularly like the scene either. His eyes were cold.

The man laying in the bed could've been ten years older than our dad. He looked worn. His skin was very pale and there were drops of sweat along his hairline. Everything about him looked fragile. He turned his head to watch us. He gave a weak nod and his head dropped back down to his pillow.

This man couldn't be far from death's door. Here in front of me was a prime example of what years of heavy drinking would do to you. All that was left was the shell of a man. He didn't look like he was alive when he closed his eyes. The only indication that his heart was still beating was the steady beeping coming from the monitor beside him.

A nurse walked in and jumped a little when she saw us. She looked from us to the bed.

"I'm sorry," she said softly. "I didn't realize we had gotten a hold of any family members. We had tried different numbers, but there was never an answer while I was there." She told us she would get the doctor and excused herself from the room.

No one moved or said a word. My insides were screaming to do something. To say the things I had come here to say. All of the words felt thick in my throat. No one else had answered any of the calls from the hospital. His family had left him.

A tired doctor walked into the room. He looked like he had been up all night. Then he looked at Dad. Maybe it was just me, but I thought the doctor looked displeased. He walked over to mom and shook her hand, then stopped.

"Do I know you?" He asked.

"Yes I work here. Usually I'm around the front desk." she replied.

"Ah, is this your husband?"

"My ex-husband." She strained to say.

"Well, I'm sorry to say he had quite a rough night. One too many drinks will do this to you. He suffered a heart attack, but we also found that his liver and kidneys are shutting down." The doctor still sounded annoyed. Maybe he didn't like treating drunks. He would've preferred helping a patient who actually needed him, not one who had done themselves in this way.

"Is there any chance he'll make it?" Gabriel was the one to ask. He hadn't moved. He didn't look up. His eyes still burned a hole through the man in the bed. And the man stared right back at him.

"We could go in and fix things, but at this point, it might do more harm than good. It seems like everything struck at once."

Gabriel's eyes finally move away from the degraded creature on the bed, and he looks at the doctor. He gives a slight nod of his head. The doctor stands there a moment longer. Checking his watch he must decide that there are other places he is needed and hurries from the room.

Gabriel looks like he wants to put a hole through the wall. He sits in a chair and holds his arms out to Anna. Sobbing loudly, she goes over to him and climbs onto his lap. The only person in the room crying is Anna. I look over at my mother. She is looking at the floor. We are the only ones in the room not knowing how to express our feelings about the situation. I try to work through the emotions in the silence.

"I'm going to go for a walk." Mom says. "Do whatever needs to be done." She backs out of the room keeping her eyes on Gabriel. Right before she was gone, her eyes swept to the figure on the bed. There would be no tears for him.

Dad looked at us. For the first time he looked like he was alert. I know he had listened to everything that was said while we were here. It was almost easy to forget that he was able to listen.

"Well," I started. My voice was even and it caught my siblings attention. "We came here to say some things. May as well say them. This may have been a surprise way to do it, but we should do it none the less."

Anna got up and walked over to the bed. She touched the skin of his arm and whimpered. She might not love him, but I felt bad. This still had to be hard on her.

149

"Daddy?" She said in a small voice. "Daddy, you're gonna die?"

Memories flashed through my head. I was barely in the room anymore. My mind played out each memory like a small movie. Each one was a slap in the face, threatening to break me and make me cry.

I remembered screaming at my dad one night for calling me princess. He had always called me that. I was his little princess. He showed me that was a lie though. I wasn't a princess, and I wasn't his. Being called princess was like being punched in the face over and over.

I had made him cry that night. It wasn't good for anyone. I'm pretty sure his princess died that night. He was left with me. A daughter he could barely look in the eyes. I wasn't his princess. I was probably his nightmare.

Another memory crashed through my head. Anna being tossed up on the roof as a little girl to retrieve a frisbee. Another, playing baseball together in the backyard and Gabriel drilling the ball into Dad's stomach.

Anna came over to me. She was still crying. I didn't want her to have to listen to all of the things Gabriel and I would say. If she had any happy memories, I wanted her to keep them.

"Go find mommy okay hun? Walk with her. Tell her Gabe and I will come find you both shortly.

As soon as she left, Gabriel sighed. He moved uncomfortably in his seat. His words came out slow and only loud enough so that Dad could hear them.

"You know, as a kid, I always thought we had a pretty good connection. That we were the kind of father and son you saw on the T.V. We went fishing, we played ball, we went deer spotting. You never see the father and son behind the scenes though. Nothing really meant much to you did it?" He paused, but not long enough for a response. "If we really had meant something to you, you would still be there. Go ahead, say you care all you want. I'm not a kid, and I'm not stupid. You do not show that you care." Gabriel's voice started shaking towards the end.

"I know what it's like to be loved by a parent. Not from you, but mom. You even tried taking that away from me. What you did is beyond wrong. I always wished that you would realize it by yourself, but it seems like you didn't." After this he left the room.

I sat there for a while not speaking. It was us. Alone to talk. Something I always wanted. To say what was on mind without anyone judging it. When I looked up at my dad his eyes were closed, and I thought he was already gone.

I started to get up and then jumped when he spoke.

"Aren't you gonna break me down too princess?"

I froze and looked back at him. Of all the things he could've said.

I walked a couple steps closer and gritted my teeth.

"I didn't come here to break you. I wanted you to finally admit to what you did. You tried to kill our mom. Your own wife. You scarred your children for life. I think Gabriel got that point across." My voice was still calm. I felt in control. "You aren't going to hurt us anymore." I whispered.

I was waiting for the tears, but they weren't coming. I was done. For me this was over. He laid there laughing at me. Maybe he was losing his mind too.

"I really screwed up," he said. "take care of your family Hope." He closed his eyes and rest his head against the pillow. Something seemed to be missing. I looked around the room. Finally I noticed the screen shoving our Dad's heart rate. The line wasn't moving. There were no beeps. Only one low whine to say that he was gone.

I walked away and considered getting a nurse. I decided against it. No doubt they would be coming soon anyways. I walked towards the door and stopped.

Turning my head, I said my goodbye. "I have my closure. This is my freedom from my pain. This is your freedom from yours. Bye Dad."

Walking down the hall two nurses and the doctor were running down the hall to the room. I didn't stop them to tell them they were too late. They would know once they got there.

It's over.

Chapter 14

I look up at the door. There are my children and my ex-wife. My angel came after all. I have a feeling she won't stay though. I know the reason they are here. It isn't to say goodbye or to mourn me. They came to cut me to pieces.

The doctor comes in and talks to them. I can't understand most of the words. Honestly, I don't care either way. I'm not leaving this place again. I watch the expressions on the faces of the people in the room instead.

Then I want to hear what's going on. The doctor has left. The haze clears a bit. Poor little Anna comes over and whispers her goodbye to me. Then Gabriel. The words, he's no doubt practiced, cut me to my core. I look at my son. He isn't a little boy anymore. He's grown up

"...not from you but from mom." He says harshly. After he's finished, he leaves the room like Anna did.

Sharp pain floods throughout my body. I close my eyes. I hear Hope get up to leave. Doesn't she have anything to say? Won't she cut me to pieces too?

"Aren't you gonna break me too princess?" I ask.

The way she responds surprises me. It's not the cutting words I expect. She'd grown up also. Enough to see her cold logic almost hurts more than her wanting me to suffer.

I tell her to take care of her family. I barely get it out before my heart cuts out. I can't feel it beat in my chest anymore. I close my eyes and go to sleep one last time. I feel one piece of me, my soul, pull away from my body. I'm gone.

It's over.

Chapter 15

The house is quiet. There isn't anything more to be said. Dad's mother finally came forward to take care of the funeral arrangements. Few attended, and those who had wished they wouldn't have. We all watch our mother. She doesn't seem to have much reaction to it. She's still probably trying to figure out how she feels. As much as this was my freedom, it was hers too.

Gabriel looked lost and confused the first day. After a week he recovered. Anna would sit and flip through old pictures. I wonder how she feels. She hasn't cried the past few days.

I'm thinking about him being judged by God. I wonder if he can hear me right now. If he can, I have some input for his decision. *He never said sorry.*

Chapter 16

Can it all have really happened? Could it have happened so fast? I look in the mirror. Hope is right. I look and feel lost. I look at Anna and see sorrow. I don't know how Hope feels.

I don't feel sadness. It feels like Dad was erased from our lives. No one talks about it. Sometimes I think Anna wants to, but can't find the words to say.

One night I walk into the kitchen and find Hope with a cup of tea. I go and get myself one and then sit down next to her.

"Are you sad?" I ask quietly.

"In a way yes, and in a way no. I'm not really sure. I know I should be sad, but I kinda feel like this is what was meant to happen. Maybe something like this would've happened regardless. I feel somewhat stupid. I never asked my questions." She said. "I'm pretty sure I know the answers though. Just by looking at him. They were there in his eyes."

She doesn't feel right about it either.

"Should we be sad?" She whispers.

"I don't know. Whatever we feel we feel. Doesn't change anything now." I pause giving her time to think. "Hope, we tried. We didn't fail at what we set out to do.

"How did we win?"

"You already answered that yourself. He made the acknowledgment that he hurt us. He took responsibility for it even if he didn't say he was sorry that he did it."

Anna came in. I wondered how long she had been listening. She crawled onto my lap, and I put my arms around her. The little girl who kept fighting for a dad had given up.

After a while, Mom walked in and found us together asleep on the couch. She came up behind us and wrapped her arms around us.

"I love you all." She said

I got up and walked around. Putting my arms around her I said, "we all love you too mom. Always have, and always will." I held her while she cried.

"Don't worry Mom. It's over."

Epilogue

I keep walking. Finally I get to a fork in the road. I sit on top of a big boulder that divides the paths. One path goes up into the sky, and the other drops deep into the ground. I get to decide my fate? Heaven or Hell?

I walk up the path where Heaven will be waiting for me at the end. I walk away from the dark path that leads to the sound of horrible screams. Screams that end in choked gurgles.

The walk seems to take forever. When I finally reach the end of the path, it feels as if the beauty has knocked the wind out of me. This truly is Heaven. I go over to the beautiful golden gates. I try to open them. I miss the metal completely. Every time I try to grab on, my hand passes right through the gold.

Laughter floats down around me. Angels are shaking their heads. Why are they laughing? Why are they up there mocking me? I go for the gate again. I'm blinded by a white light as I'm electrocuted. My skin is black and charred. It flakes off in tiny pieces. I walk backwards away from the cruel gates. As I take another step back, I realize the path is gone. I'm falling down through the air.

The angels taunt me. They point and laugh. All but one. He sits there looking disappointed. He has no wings. He shakes his head slowly as I fall.

I plummet through the air. The screams are getting louder as I fall faster. The screams of the damned flood my ears. I land hard on my back. It is so dark. The only light comes from a black door. The light burns behind it.

I feel my heart stop as I watch the knob turn slowly. I back away as far as I can, but I am trapped in this pit. The door opens slowly. It gets warmer. The fires of Hell dance in the opening. A huge creature with black leathery wings comes forth.

The large black wings shoot out, and I see their full size. The monster shrieks. Scratches and burns litter the beings flesh.

It comes for me in no hurry knowing I'm trapped. I beg for mercy. My pleading falls on deaf ears. I'm grabbed and slowly drug through the door.

I try to fight. I kick and scream. It's no use. I shriek in fear. The door closes behind me. My voice is lost. It's just another addition in the chorus of the damned. I am just another resident in Hell.

About the Author

Natalie Rose Kohuth lives in Wyano, PA with her mother Sherry, and her younger brother Alex.

Natalie is currently a Junior at Yough High School, and plans to attend college to pursue a career in Psychiatry. She is actively involved in softball, track, cross country, the high school musical, and in her 14th year of dance.

Made in the USA
Middletown, DE
09 August 2023

36441292R00099